COMMITMENT TO EXCELLENCE

The Remarkable Amway Story

Wilbur Cross   Gordon Olson

COMMITMENT TO EXCELLENCE

The Remarkable Amway Story

BENJAMIN

Research and original manuscript: Gordon Olson

Library of Congress Catalog Card Number: 85-73071

ISBN: 0-87502-136-0

Produced and published for Amway Corporation
                    by The Benjamin Company, Inc.
                    One Westchester Plaza
                    Elmsford, New York 10523

First Printing: November 1986

CONTENTS

Gerald R. Ford, 38th President of the United States

Foreword

I HEAR AMERICA SINGING

"I hear America singing,
the varied carols I hear ...
Singing with open mouths
their strong melodious songs."
— Walt Whitman

"I hear America singing, the varied carols I hear ...."
So began one of the nation's greatest poets, Walt Whitman, in a paean of rejoicing at the spirit and dedication of Americans at work, whether at a lathe or a plow, in a kitchen or tending children, on a steamboat deck or traveling the open road.

Were Whitman alive today, I think he would exult in the fact that there are still Americans who are exuberant in their work, free and independent in their outlook, and able to go about their jobs with a song in their hearts and a feeling of rapport with the people they serve. Nowhere in America are the lines he penned more than a century ago so applicable as in the spirit that pervades the people who have committed themselves to Amway.

I have known Jay Van Andel and Rich DeVos for many years, going back to the days when I was a United States Congressman from Michigan. I have watched their business grow and spread from our home state right across the United States, north into Canada, and around the world. I have taken a deep personal interest in Amway's accomplishments. More importantly, I have been proud of the way in which the company has become one of the prime representatives of the free enterprise system in many lands and among many peoples.

The thousands of Amway distributorships are dramatic proof that the American spirit of free enterprise is, and will continue to be, a vibrant force at home and abroad. Every distributor is, in effect, an ambassador, earning respect and support for the democratic way of life. When we acknowledge the success of Amway, we are really showing our support for the American concept of doing business. A free enterprise economy can only exist under the patronage of a free government.

That is what Amway has meant to me over the years, as Congressman, as President, and as an American citizen. I can only say to Rich DeVos and Jay Van Andel that I hope Amway goes on forever, attracting the peoples of the world to a better way of life and bringing new hope for the future.

— GERALD R. FORD

Rich DeVos and Jay Van Andel, as depicted in the Paul Collins 25th Anniversary Mural "The Bond."

Chapter One

AUSPICIOUS BEGINNINGS

*"What man's age is like to be
doth show; We may by our
beginnings know."*
— *John Denham*

It was the year that Alaska and Hawaii were admitted as the 49th and 50th states; that the long-planned St. Lawrence Seaway was opened; that the N.S. *Savannah,* the world's first nuclear-powered merchant ship, was launched; that the hit musical *Flower Drum Song,* by Rodgers and Hammerstein, was charming Broadway;

It was the year that Soviet Premier Nikita Khrushchev paid an unprecedented visit to the United States and toured the country from East to West; that NASA selected the first seven astronauts to train for journeys to outer space;

It was 1959, the year in which a seemingly modest, unheralded event also took place — yet one that was to shape the lives and life-styles of millions of people in a manner that was not dreamed of by even the participants themselves.

It was the year that Amway was born.

A decade or so earlier two young entrepreneurs, Jay Van Andel and Richard DeVos, had established a network of independent direct-selling distributors. These longtime friends and business partners were enjoying modest success marketing Nutrilite® Food Supplements, developed by Nutrilite Products, Inc., a California-based company.

Nutrilite was a multi-vitamin, multi-mineral supplement formulated from concentrate made from specially grown alfalfa, watercress, and parsley, plus yeast, minerals, and vitamins. It had been developed by Carl Rehnborg, owner of the Nutrilite company, and was a new concept in food supplements at that time.

During the first full year, 1950, their sales organization had grossed $82,000, followed by a four-fold increase the next year. By 1954, the "Ja-Ri" (from their first names and pronounced "jah-ree") sales network had fanned across southern Michigan and into Ohio and Illinois.

However, Nutrilite sales started to slacken in the second half of the 1950s as increasing government regulation radically limited the claims that could be made about nutritional products. By 1958, frustration had mounted to where Nutrilite Products (manufacturer of the food supplement) and Mytinger and Castleberry (national distributor for Nutrilite) locked horns over the future of the business. Nutrilite, exploring ways to recover lost sales volume, was considering production of a cosmetics line; Mytinger and Castleberry raised fervent opposition. Nutrilite's success, they argued, depended on a dedicated salesperson whose enthusiatic presentation reflected belief in the product; that enthusiasm would dissipate if spread over several product lines.

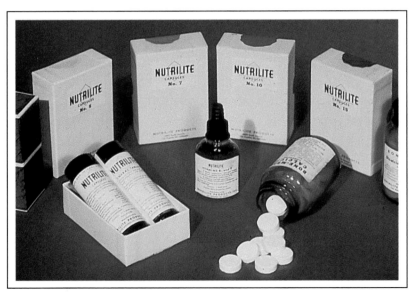

The talks reached a flash point when the two companies launched competitive product lines. Mytinger and Castleberry began to manufacture and offer to the distributors their own brand of cosmetics; Nutrilite brought out the "Edith Rehnborg" cosmetics line and circumvented Mytinger and Castleberry by selling it direct to the distributors.

Matters reached a deadlock when Nutrilite Products decided to sever their business ties to Mytinger and Castleberry. Aware of Ja-Ri's sales record and Van Andel's work as a mediator in the dispute, Nutrilite invited the Michigan man to come to California to head their new distribution network.

"I was flattered," admits Van Andel, "and promised to give the offer 'careful consideration.' However, since I was not interested in working for someone else, I knew my chances of acceptance were slim."

BIRTH OF A VENTURE

In one way, the offer helped to break through the business stalemate and point the way to the future. After discussing the implications, Rich DeVos and Jay Van Andel told themselves: If a company as substantial as Nutrilite was confident that one of the two partners could direct a national sales, distribution, and marketing program, then it made sense that the Ja-Ri team could do just as well on its own — probably better.

In the early spring of 1959, Van Andel, DeVos, and seven leading distributors in the Ja-Ri sales force traveled to the little town of Charlevoix in northern Michigan. It was imperative to discuss the future of the business that they, and several thousand other distributors, depended upon for all or part of their livelihoods.

PIONEER TRAILS: TOP, Carl Rehnborg, founder of Nutrilite Products, Inc. CENTER, harvest day in 1956 for the specially grown grains used in Nutrilite Food Supplements. BOTTOM, Nutrilite's mid-1940s product line.

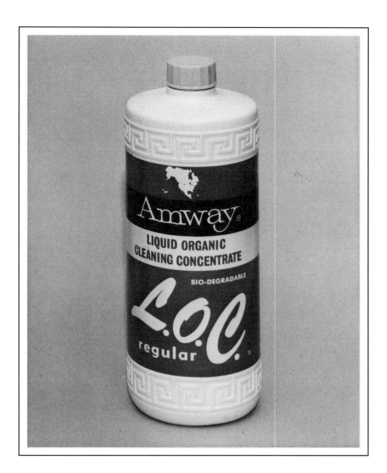

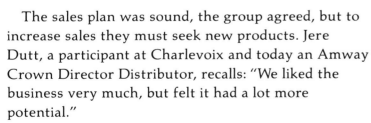

FIRST STEPS: *ABOVE AND TOP RIGHT, early package designs for Amway's first two products, L.O.C.® Cleaner and S-A-8™ Laundry Detergent. BOTTOM RIGHT, young entrepreneur Jay Van Andel outside the corporate offices of the fledgling Ja-Ri Corporation.*

The sales plan was sound, the group agreed, but to increase sales they must seek new products. Jere Dutt, a participant at Charlevoix and today an Amway Crown Director Distributor, recalls: "We liked the business very much, but felt it had a lot more potential."

"When you can recruit only specially skilled people," said Jay Van Andel, "you will necessarily limit the size of your sales force. The products we want must, first of all, be ones that just about anyone is familiar with and can sell. They have to meet two criteria: be of such nature that the government is not going to severely regulate what you say about them in your sales efforts; and be something that people need, and *know* that they need, without having to be convinced. The examples that come to mind are laundry and cleaning products."

As the Charlevoix meeting made clear, a fundamental requirement for the success of Nutrilite lay in wholehearted approval from everyone in selling. "The situation was sensitive and required careful handling," said DeVos later. "Our distributors were divided in their loyalties: appreciative of Ja-Ri and its sponsorship, but understandably faithful to the Nutrilite product that they sold so successfully. For many of them, selling Nutrilite had become a mission, not just a means to a profit. They used the product themselves, found it beneficial, and wanted to tell the world about it."

"We couldn't expect our distributors to transfer that kind of missionary zeal to a box of laundry soap," Van Andel recalls wryly, "but they had enough confidence in us to express a willingness to *try.*"

"We had all the confidence in the world in Jay and Rich," says Crown Direct Distributor Bernice Hansen, one of the distributors attending the conference, "and we were willing to follow them. They had proved their worth. They had never hedged on a promise or violated a principle."

Buoyed by this new spirit of action and optimism, DeVos and Van Andel scheduled a second meeting for that spring. This time, on April 23, they met at the Hotel Leland in Detroit, along with the key distributors who had attended the first conference.

The most conspicuous result was the formation of a distributor association with a board of directors comprised of DeVos, Van Andel, and seven other members, all chosen by annual vote.

Elected as the first president of the new association was Walter Bass, an active distributor in Ja-Ri who was considered an outstanding spokesman for his colleagues.

With the drafting of its bylaws, the association was a reality. The fundamental question, "What are we going to sell?", was now asked repeatedly. A small test was run with a unique car wash product.

Then, throughout the fall of 1959, a biodegradable liquid detergent was tested, along with other products that included furniture polish, an oven cleaner, a copper cleaner, and a laundry detergent that were manufactured by small Michigan firms.

By late September, DeVos and Van Andel had established the Amway Sales Corporation and Amway Services Corporation to provide the products and services (ranging from a health plan to sales literature) to the distributors who were members of the association.

The company location was officially Grand Rapids, but most of the initial action took place at the homes of the founders in Ada, Michigan.

"*A SCRAMBLING PERIOD*": OPPOSITE, TOP, *S-A-8, key item in the new Amway Corporation's product line.* OPPOSITE, BOTTOM, *Van Andel at work in Ja-Ri's Grand Rapids' offices.* ABOVE, *Ja-Ri co-founders DeVos and Van Andel, with leading members of the Nutrilite sales force.* RIGHT, *early products and friendly faces light up a 1959 Amway fair booth.*

COPING WITH GROWING PAINS

As more and more distributors joined the organization and the multi-product business burgeoned, the company passed a small, but essential, milestone: the hiring of its first full-time employee. She was Kay Evans, who had been working on a part-time basis since February 1959, handling bookkeeping and correspondence amid a clutter of office furniture and file cabinets in Van Andel's basement. This locale was one of a pair of "headquarters," the other being the DeVos basement, a few hundred feet away.

The DeVos part of the operation was administered by another part-timer, Bob Rooker, later to be appointed Amway's Director of Shift Operations. After a day spent working for the local gas company, Rooker would descend to the netherworld of distribution, unloading shipments and filling orders,

PERPETUAL MOTION: Jay Van Andel's basement, one of Amway's first "headquarters," formed the center of most day-to-day activities in the bustling new business. ABOVE, Echo St. John. BELOW (left to right), Echo St. John, Ada Denkema, Kay Evans.

using the DeVos washing machine and dryer as a convenient waist level packing area. On Saturdays, he ran the mimeograph machine, stocking the shelves with product information sheets and sales manuals written by Van Andel.

Despite the confinement and clutter, the two makeshift headquarters were characterized by an energetic pace and an optimistic attitude that boded well for the future. On one occasion, Rooker recalls, when the supply of shipping cartons was depleted, he had to pack containers of detergent in shipping cartons hastily purchased by DeVos from a local dog-food company. Not the slightest bit fazed at the receipt of cases marked "Dog Food," the distributors applauded the ingenuity and persistence of their fledgling organization, as well as the popular products and prompt service emanating from Amway's offices.

Jay Van Andel and Rich DeVos worked tirelessly to assure this kind of support. It was evident in the industrious activities taking place in the basements, in their constant contacts with the growing army of distributors, and in the perpetual motion that characterized their visits to locations throughout the Midwest.

"In the beginning," recalls Kay Evans, "they were both *outside* men. One would be in Lansing or Detroit during the day, while the other would take off to hold a meeting at night, and they'd meet midway to discuss the business."

"Loving support" was the glue that held the business together during the day-to-day crises that commonly plague so many fledgling private enterprises. Both of the founders had married in the early 1950s and were fortunate to have wives who were eager to share the load, especially during the increasingly demanding Nutrilite years. But now, there were new family responsibilities — Nan and Stephen born to the Van Andels and Richard Jr. and Daniel to the DeVoses.

Yet, even with their growing duties at home, Betty Van Andel and Helen DeVos found time to host business meetings, entertain visiting distributors and suppliers, and pitch in when extra hands were needed to fill product orders on time.

BURSTING AT THE SEAMS: Amidst the cheerful clutter of the Van Andel "basement headquarters," Rich DeVos's father, Si, takes a moment to breathe.

BUILDING AN INVENTORY: Ada's old Masonic Temple, called into service in 1960 as sometime warehouse for the growing Amway Corporation.

"When a group of distributors arrived at a predetermined goal," explains Helen DeVos, "we'd invite them to a special dinner and cook up a storm. And what we couldn't quite put together, we'd go out and buy. We had a great time socializing with our top achievers, and hoped that such recognition would help spur them on to their next goal."

Betty recalls the time they cooked a spaghetti dinner, although neither she nor Helen knew how to prepare it. It ended up as a gluey mass, unservable. Another time they made chili — but got their measurements wrong and made so much they were serving it to the families from the freezer for a year thereafter.

There seemed to be no end to the new members of the Amway "family" and the visitors who descended into the two basement offices. However, the available space quickly decreased as the size of the work force increased.

"It seemed," chuckles Kay Evans, "that more desks and shelves were being moved in every day, along with visitors. It wasn't unusual to have so many people in Jay's basement at the same time that you had to speak out whenever you wanted to change position. If you were going to move from your desk, you had to tell four or five others that you wanted out. There just wasn't any more space."

By late 1959, with space for Amway's sales and service divisions bursting at the seams, temporary relief was gained through leasing a vacant former post office in Ada and converting it into a warehouse. Six months later, Van Andel and DeVos purchased an abandoned service station down the road to house an office and some basic warehousing and shipping operations.

Carole Sandy, who joined Amway in that period of fast-paced growth, recalled a momentous day in October 1960, when Rich DeVos bounded down his

COZY QUARTERS: The converted service station in Ada, Michigan, that became Amway's first outside office building.

basement stairs and interrupted the beehive of activity.

"Come on, gang," he announced, "we're moving!" Before they knew what was happening, he had pulled his station wagon up to the back door and was recruiting everyone in sight to help move desks, file cabinets, and other furnishings and equipment. Not everything went to the new quarters — just the warehouse activities from the DeVos basement went at first. Soon the small printing machine from the Van Andel basement was moved, allowing more office expansion there.

Space shortage was not the only problem that resulted from Amway's vigorous growth. Within a year of the company's birth, it was dealing with some 15 independent suppliers, most of whom were small manufacturers who could not always deliver on time or supply the quantities required. Worse yet, they had difficulties with quality control, sometimes delivering products that fell short of Amway's strict standards, or in packaging that was inconsistent. To conduct business properly — as well as profitably — it was vital to keep products flowing in a steady stream, without interruptions caused by delayed shipments, returns, and undue warehousing.

"Amway is handling a maximum of volume on a minimum of capital," wrote Jay Van Andel in a memorandum to distributors, "so we must be cautious about tying up more capital than we can afford in any one product, while finding ourselves in short supply elsewhere."

To meet increasing consumer demand and assure reliable distribution, Amway leased six contract warehouses that were strategically located in Michigan, Illinois, Indiana, and Ohio. However, Van Andel reminded their distributors, building up these reserve stocks required extra capital. The answer: "*Sell more* and we can stock more; increased volume increases profits, which in turn allow increased inventories."

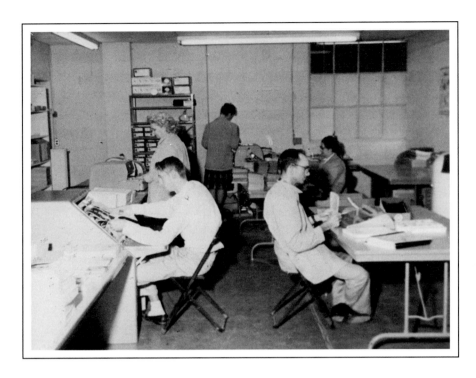

SWINGING INTO THE 60s: ABOVE, early mailroom employees keep the lines of communication open. BELOW, a steady stream of products flows to the expanding distributor network from Amway's shipping department.

THE DO-IT-YOURSELF APPROACH

As is often the case with a new business that counts on outside assistance, one supplier proved to be more consistent and reliable than the others in matters of quantity and quality alike. This was the Atco Manufacturing Company, which had diligently filled orders for one of Amway's first products, Liquid Organic Cleaner, commonly known and registered as L.O.C.® Cleaner. By contrast, other suppliers were constantly offering DeVos and Van Andel excuses for being inconsistent in product quality or tardy in delivery.

There was one sure solution to the nagging problem: *Do it yourself!* After all, both founders had a long history of taking the initiative, ranging from selling and marketing to writing promotional literature, recruiting, setting up files, transporting merchandise, lugging heavy equipment, bargaining with vendors, and even making and installing signs. There were two prospective manufacturing specialists they could solicit for help: John E. Kennedy and Eugene Slaby, business partners who headed up the little Atco Manufacturing Company.

Would Kennedy and Slaby sell a half-interest in Atco and move to the converted service station in Ada, where they would operate as Amway Manufacturing Corporation? Slaby preferred not to make the move, but agreed to sell his share of the business to his partner. Thus, Kennedy became the first manager of the new in-house manufacturing operation in November 1960, a position he was to hold for eight years until retiring and selling his shares in the manufacturing division of the business.

Although the remodeled building contained floor space of only 40 by 60 feet, it was further cramped by the addition of a print shop. Operating the small printing press and a mimeograph machine was young Wally Buttrick, then a high-school student and one of the growing legion of part-timers who were proving that a successful business could be founded on personal initiative, dedication, and loyalty. He is a fine example, too, of the way a business built by such people rewards them with personal success and fulfillment. In Buttrick's case, after spending many long hours printing the two distributor periodicals,

Amagram and *Newsgram*, product literature, and sales manuals, he rose through company ranks to become sales manager and then left to devote all his time to a thriving Amway distributorship.

Looking at that first modest headquarters and cramped manufacturing site, the small group of people involved with production, sales, and services could never have conceived that their loyalty and commitment would one day help the young company to expand into a billion-dollar organization familiar to people throughout the Western World.

The members of this dedicated group were increasingly amazed as they saw their seemingly tireless efforts, and those of the expanding distributor network, result in more sales. Not only did the orders keep flowing in, but the product lines continued to expand. Amway was now in a favorable position where it had enough flexibility and capital to experiment with new merchandise, such as water softeners, car-care products, stainless steel cookware, and at one time even a fallout shelter.

"We were always scrambling," recalls Rich DeVos, "just trying to catch up with back orders, working to train people adequately. We didn't have much time to look down the road; we were too busy meeting the demands of the day."

At the end of 1960, the company's first complete year of operation, gross sales totaled $500,000, a figure that was to double during each of the next two years and then make breathtaking leaps in the years to come.

This was Amway, swinging into the decade of the sixties. The company was dynamic, exciting, vibrant, and, in the eyes of the casual observer, brand new. Yet the fact is that the roots of the company were not new at all, but had been formed and nurtured many years earlier in the persons of the two founders. History is built on history, strength on strength, durability on durability — essentials that were there from the very beginning.

VITAL SIGNS: Wally Buttrick from the Sales Department presents an optimistic forecast to an early 1960s PSIE (Product and Sales Idea Evaluation Committee).

Campau Square, downtown Grand Rapids, circa 1935.

Chapter Two

PIONEERS ON FAR TRAILS

"Once a relatively few
pioneers followed far trails
through the American
wilderness. Today there are
millions of people who are
determined to leave their huts
and their poverty behind
them."
— *Herbert Victor Prochnow*

Grand Rapids, Michigan, in the mid-1930s was a classic example of a Middle American community striving to survive the Depression. It was a city searching for a range of economic resources to keep people in jobs, and betting on the grit and determination of its citizens, many of them of resolute Dutch stock, to see their way through to a more promising future. Although one of the important segments of the city's industry was rooted in furniture making, its economy was substantially diversified in truck farming, communications, education, paper processing, and manufacturing.

It was in this environment, in the west central region of Michigan's Lower Peninsula, that Jay Van Andel and Richard DeVos were born (in 1924 and 1926 respectively) and raised. In school, they learned something about the Dutch heritage of the region, passed down to their families, whose roots were in Holland. They heard accounts of the Ottawa Indians who had inhabited the Lower Peninsula at the time a fur trading post and a historic mission were

established in 1826 on the site that would soon be known as Grand Rapids.

As young boys, they felt many of the restrictions of the Great Depression, living in a world where they were brought up to "waste not" and to practice the little economies that saved electricity, water, and gas; to get by with mended knickers instead of new ones; and to expect quite a few of their meals to be made up of leftovers prepared in ingenious ways. Although their own fathers were constantly struggling to make ends meet, they managed to retain just enough independence to be better off than many of their neighbors. Many were laid off, sometimes by companies they had given years of loyal service.

In many cases, the fathers of their friends were trying to hold out against forces beyond their control, hanging on to their pride in their determination to earn their own way without accepting handouts. They expected to work their way through the bleak times. A good many families who really needed help simply refused to accept it.

Depression layoffs drove home one important point that was to affect the future of the two boys deeply and directly: *The man who had to depend upon an employer for a living could never be sure of his next paycheck.*

"My father went through life frustrated that he'd never had a business of his own," recalls Rich DeVos. "He talked so often about owning and operating his own business that it was a continuing message to me and I never thought seriously about a career that required working for someone else."

The young Van Andel was slightly more fortunate. Though far from being wealthy, his family fared better than most. "My father started a number of business ventures," he explains, "including an automobile dealership he opened in 1932 — during the depths of the Depression. Yet it survived and he still operates it today. It demonstrated one significant business principle to me: The time to start an enterprise is when *you* are ready. You don't let the economic environment dictate your course of action — you just go ahead and take the plunge."

AN IMPORTANT LINK

As fate would have it, this independent venture, the formation of the auto dealership, was what led to the first "partnership" between Jay Van Andel and Richard DeVos. Thanks to his father's business, Van Andel was able to drive to high school in a Model "A" Ford roadster. When the Van Andels built a new house on the northeast end of Grand Rapids, it was close to the home of Rich DeVos, who quickly noticed the roadster, and with good reason. It was being used to drive several miles to a private school, Christian High, which he also attended.

Seeing an alternative to pedaling his balloon-tired bicycle over a route that was demanding in good weather and treacherous in bad, the enterprising DeVos proposed an arrangement that would benefit them both: He would pay Van Andel 25¢ a week for daily transportation to and from school. Van Andel accepted the offer and discovered, during the ensuing commute, that he shared many ideas and interests with the younger DeVos. Soon they were chumming around after school hours and beginning to talk about the possibilities of one day launching their own business.

That enterprise was still several years distant when Van Andel graduated from Christian High and enrolled in Calvin College, also located nearby in Grand Rapids. In the meantime DeVos devoted so much time to extracurricular activities that "my folks finally concluded that I just wasn't cut out for study and transferred me to a technical high school." That experience proved so unbearable that DeVos offered to pay his own tuition if he could transfer back to Christian High. The net result was that he returned to Christian High (his parents paid the tuition). He learned enough from this experience to see to it that he greatly improved his study habits. No threat to the class valedictorian, he was nevertheless a popular student leader and graduated as president of his senior class.

The early 1940s brought about wide disruptions in the plans of young people trying to look beyond the school doors and into the future. Hitler's Germany and Hirohito's Japan cast their dark shadows as much over America's heartland as over any region in the United States, where people of all ages joined in aiding the war effort. Hoping to complete his studies, Van Andel joined the Enlisted Reserve Corps, but soon was called to active duty. Fortunately, his enlistment gave him the privilege of selecting his branch of service. He chose the Army Air Corps and was assigned to the cadet school at Yale University, where he received his commission as an Air Force officer.

"It was the most impressive learning experience I'd ever had," he said later. "The intensive training, in competition with some of the brightest students in the country, and requiring attendance at classes that frequently started at 4:30 A.M., brought out qualities I never quite realized I possessed."

FROM TINY ACORNS: TOP, the first Amway Distributors Convention, held in Grand Rapids in 1961. BOTTOM LEFT, James and Nella Van Andel with son Jay. BOTTOM CENTER, friends of the Van Andel family gather around the Model "A" Ford that Jay (on roof) would soon be driving back and forth to Christian High. BOTTOM RIGHT, father and son Si and Rich DeVos.

DeVos also selected the Army Air Corps, enlisting at the time of his graduation from Christian High. He was assigned to Shepard Field in Wichita Falls, Texas. Through correspondence, the two friends traded military anecdotes, often lightheartedly, but sometimes taking serious jabs at their common object of scorn: military bureaucracy. On a more productive note, they shared an impatience to see the war over so they could become their own bosses; and they were both convinced this exciting new world of flying would play a vital role in postwar America.

THE REWARDS OF INITIATIVE

The first of the two friends to be discharged, Van Andel returned to Grand Rapids, where he found his and DeVos's enthusiasm for flying echoed in widespread public interest. "It was a time," he recalls, "in which the whole country seemed convinced that there would soon be two airplanes in every garage and you would fly wherever you went — even down to the nearby shopping centers."

He discussed aviation's popularity with a friend who had also served in the Air Corps, both concluding that the best way to get in on the ground floor would be to purchase their own small plane. He proposed the idea to DeVos, still in service, and received not only a vote of confidence, but a small sum saved from Rich's military pay. Thus it was that, with $700 in pooled resources, the three men invested in a Piper Cub and opened a flying school.

It so happened that, while they had been looking for a good bargain in aircraft, they had met another aviation enthusiast who harbored a desire to build an airport on an old fairgrounds north of Grand Rapids. If they would all join forces to offer basic training and charter flights, they could be in business with a very low investment. The idea appealed and the Wolverine Air Service was born, its name inspired by the state's nickname.

After more than five years of planning for the day when they could be partners in their own business, DeVos and Van Andel had finally achieved the beginnings of what they hoped could truly be the Great American Dream. It was not to be quite that soon or quite that easy. Yet it was an auspicious start.

With one airplane, limited capital, and boundless faith in themselves and in each other, they had embarked on the first of a series of ventures which, over the next 15 years, would refine the business skills and economic clarity needed for their ultimate achievement: Amway Corporation.

This initial enterprise verified the importance of one key to success: being in the right place with the right service at the right time. Even though the anticipated "two-plane family" was a rarity, the popularity of flying began to blossom, nourished in part by the enthusiasm of young men and women who had been exposed to flight during World War II. The idea of soaring through the wild blue yonder so captured the American imagination that the United States Veterans Administration was persuaded to include flight training in its roster of courses eligible under the G.I. Bill of Rights. As a result, the new flying school opened its doors to a flock of eager applicants.

Wolverine Air Service had its throttle poised for flight, only to face a major obstacle in its path. Construction of the new runways had fallen behind schedule and not one was yet approved for take-off. Creativity came to the fore. The ingenious solution of the partners was to equip the plane with pontoons so it could use the nearby Grand River as a safe "landing strip" without forcing them to lose time — and much-needed income. Having quickly done their homework, the owners of Wolverine had learned that there were no regulations forbidding flight training on water. The resourceful solution gave them such a big jump on their would-be competitors that the partners were able to graduate their first student before the airport had been officially opened for service!

The young entrepreneurs soon learned another rewarding business principle: Having a good product to offer the public is not enough; that product must also be *sold*. After the initial group of students had arrived to sign up, the prospects became fewer and fewer. "We knew they were out there," admits DeVos, "but we just hadn't bothered to go out and get them." He and Van Andel wasted no time. Since neither of them was licensed to teach, they were free to spend

TAXIING FOR TAKEOFF: TOP LEFT, Lieutenant Jay Van Andel, after graduation from the Army Air Corps cadet school at Yale University. TOP RIGHT, Rich DeVos, upon completion of his Army Air Corps training. BOTTOM, one of the first planes to put Wolverine Air Service in flight.

their time soliciting new trainees while a hired instructor handled the training. As a result, Wolverine got another big jump on the competition. The competition largely depended on using their pilots to both seek out and train their enrollees.

Recruiting new students taught Van Andel and DeVos the value of conceiving a detailed sales plan with which to present their offer to potential customers. Enlisting the aid of a cooperative high-school administrator, they designed a basic ground-school academic program. This curriculum, sanctioned by the government and complementing the flight

school's air time, was the clincher in convincing potential students that Wolverine offered nothing but the most thorough instruction.

Within a few months after opening its doors, Wolverine Air Service had enrolled enough students to support a second instructor and, before long, to finance the purchase of a second plane as well. The partners did not overlook the opportunity to sell merchandise as well as services. Noting that there was no retail outlet for aviation accessories in the area, they turned one corner of their already cramped airport office into a salesroom. Soon they were selling

PROUD OWNERS: Van Andel and DeVos pose with one of their flying school's airplanes.

IF YOU CAN DRIVE A CAR - YOU CAN FLY A PLANE

WOLVERINE AIR SERVICE
GRAND RIVER AIRPARK, COMSTOCK PARK
GRAND RAPIDS, MICHIGAN

YOUNG ENTREPRENEURS: ABOVE, "Selling the Product" through a Wolverine brochure. RIGHT, Van Andel and DeVos in uniform.

flight jackets, gloves, scarves, charts, boots, insignia, and other aviation products that appealed to this specialized market.

Another need became apparent: the lack of suitable restaurants in an area that was becoming populated not only by flight students but by visitors who liked to drive out to the airport, watch the planes landing and taking off, and then find a place to eat. Ever alert to consumer needs, DeVos and Van Andel had been quite impressed when, on a business trip to California, they had enjoyed their first encounter with a drive-in restaurant. Would it work in Grand Rapids? Why not?

The outcome was the Riverside Drive-Inn, designed with a series of parking stalls where motorists could pull in, push a button for the waiter, and place their orders. The venture had only one initial drawback: The partners could not yet afford the extra help needed for peak evening hours. The solution was quite obvious: When their long work day at the flying school ended, they would put on another hat — broiling hamburgers and hot dogs and hopping cars at the drive-in.

As though this commitment were not challenging enough, the young entrepreneurs mounted a third enterprise, which seemed quite natural because of their convenient location on the Grand River. This was a boat rental business, offering radio-equipped canoes and cartop boats, available at the restaurant not far

HANDS TO THE HELM: Wolverine's young founders work out some of the numerous details attendant to their new company's growth.

from the stream's banks. By this time, assuming even more of the work load and responsibility, Van Andel and DeVos had bought out their third partner. The young man had decided that the entrepreneurial life was not for him and he was going to study to become an engineer.

The ventures into the restaurant and boat rental fields were not motivated by any slack, as yet, in the aviation business. To the contrary, Wolverine had broadened in the nature of services and expanded its sales. In addition to flight training and charter flights, Wolverine was now handling light air freight shipments, supplying gasoline and lubricants to planes passing through, and adding new services as needed.

Rich DeVos and Jay Van Andel, however, could envision a saturation point for the business, or at least a leveling off that was not in keeping with their philosophy of continual expansion. They had undeniably proved to themselves that they could prosper as a successful management team, demonstrating through practical application a flair for

analyzing problems, and coming up with shrewd, productive answers.

Many acquaintances and local businessmen were surprised when, in 1949, Van Andel and DeVos announced that they were selling their prosperous operations and moving on to other things. What outsiders did not realize at the time was that the two partners were not content with running businesses that had limited growth potential. It had become apparent that Americans were not ready yet for two planes in every garage and that owning even one was a luxury few could afford.

Observers were even more perplexed when they learned what the two young entrepreneurs were planning to embark on for their newest enterprise. With the proceeds from the sale, DeVos and Van Andel were about to demonstrate that their zeal for business could be matched by a zest for adventure.

"We closed up all our business interests in Grand Rapids," explains DeVos, "deposited part of the money in the bank, took what we needed for our next venture, and headed straight for the Caribbean."

DIVERSIFICATION: The first of its kind in Grand Rapids, the Riverside Drive-Inn proved a successful sideline to the young partners' air service business.

A SPIRIT OF INDEPENDENCE

Inspired by author, adventurer, and seafarer Dick Bertram, who had sailed to the Caribbean before World War II, DeVos and Van Andel invested in a boat of their own. She was a wooden-hulled 38-foot Nova Scotia schooner, which for some five years had languished in drydock in Norwalk, Connecticut, because of World War II.

If the ship's seagoing capabilities were open to some question, the crew's proficiencies and skills were even more so. With plans that might have fazed even an experienced skipper, they charted an ambitious course southward along the Intracoastal Waterway and the U.S. East Coast to Cuba, which at that time still enjoyed friendly relations with the United States. To their credit, they *did* reach their island destination, but only after a series of misadventures that included losing their way a few times, frequently running

aground, and constantly pumping water from what proved to be a very leaky hull.

Although the inland mariners from Michigan were applying their usual ingenuity and determination to their seagoing apprenticeship and were getting their sea legs, they had to face the dismal truth. Tender loving care and fervent prayers just were not enough to make the *Elizabeth* any more seaworthy. As she took aboard increasing amounts of saltwater, her crew realized they could press their luck no further. Sighting a small harbor on Cuba's north coast, they put in for repairs.

Two weeks later, with renewed hope, a recaulked hull underfoot, and a newly hired Cuban seaman to lend assistance, they again set sail. Hope dimmed some 50 miles from their embarkation point when the new caulking began to pop out of the planks and the schooner's pumps could not keep pace with the seawater gurgling through the seams. This time, there was no question of limping to port for repairs. It was the middle of the night, they were far from shore, and the situation was desperate.

As the waterlogged *Elizabeth* settled lower and lower in the sea, her three-man crew gave up on the pumps and devoted their energies to shooting off flares, blinking SOS signals with the ship's flashlight, and straining their eyes for lights that would reveal some approaching vessel.

About 2:30 A.M., their distress signal was sighted by the *Addabel Lykes*, an ocean transport out of New Orleans. By the time the faint light of dawn broke

over the horizon, Van Andel and DeVos were leaning over the toprail of the *Lykes*, watching their old schooner settle under the gold-tipped swells of the sea. All that remained of their Caribbean dream was a smattering of personal belongings they had saved during the rescue scramble.

Most amateur vagabonds would have decided they had experienced enough excitement and adventure and charted a more conservative course — for home. But not DeVos and Van Andel. A substantial part of their original objective had been to explore South America, and they were not going to be denied the experience. Dropped off by their rescue vessel on the hospitable, sunbaked shores of Puerto Rico, they were able to sign on as deckhands on a British tramp steamer heading for the island of Curaçao in the Dutch West Indies.

ANCHORS AWEIGH: Van Andel and DeVos en route to the Caribbean aboard the 38-foot schooner Elizabeth.

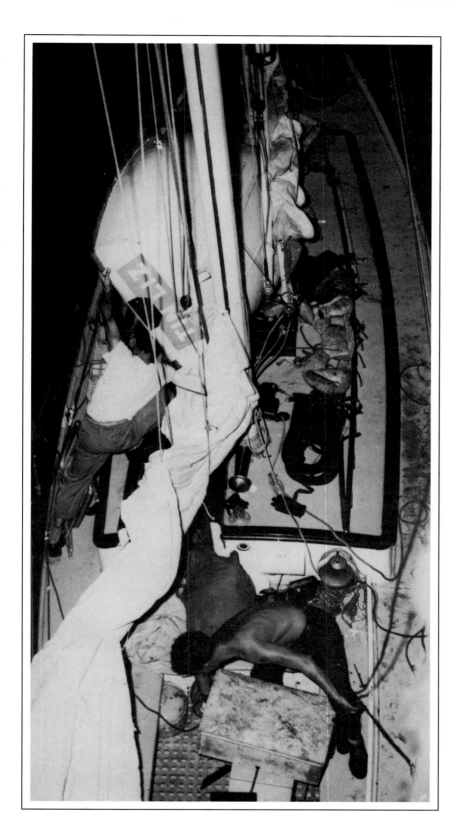

ABANDON SHIP: The Elizabeth *foundering off the shores of Cuba, as seen from the decks of her rescue vessel, the ocean transport* Addabel Lykes.

From there they flew south to Venezuela, then west to Colombia, where they secured passage on an ancient paddle-wheel steamer that took them eight hundred miles down the Magdalena River into the equatorial jungles, stopping at night with armed guards on shore. The action could have come right out of a Humphrey Bogart adventure film.

"We were just having fun," recalls Rich DeVos in an uncharacteristically low-key manner. "Seeing the world. Enjoying life. Meeting different people from unfamiliar cultures."

Sometimes purchasing fares, sometimes hitching rides or working their way, they continued their odyssey southward. A narrow-gauge railway took them from the Colombian interior to the seacoast, followed by a voyage on a freighter down South America's Pacific Coast, past Ecuador and Peru to Chile. From Santiago they flew over the Andes, at a point where the peaks top 22,000 feet, to Buenos Aires. From the Argentinian capital they flew northward to a succession of exotic places, including Montevideo, Rio de Janeiro, Surinam, Guyana, Trinidad, Antigua, and the Virgin Islands, before heading back home to Michigan.

The exciting and far-ranging travels of Rich DeVos and Jay Van Andel made news in Grand Rapids, enough so that the two partners cannily decided they could capitalize on their newly earned renown as world travelers. Assembling their colored movies, they presented travelogues to small, attentive audiences of armchair adventurers. Profit was not their only objective. Rather, they saw their presentations as a way to hone their communications skills and refine their ability to convey ideas and impressions to diverse groups of relative strangers.

They were not certain at the time just how their efforts at organizing and communicating would pay off. Yet it would come as no surprise a few years later that they had acquired both confidence and persuasiveness when they embarked on what was to be the biggest venture of all: motivating hundreds of thousands of people to join in a worldwide marketing and distribution program that would be unique in the annals of American business.

A convention in Grand Rapids for Nutrilite distributors, sponsored by the Ja-Ri distributorship in the early 1950s.

Chapter Three

THE AMWAY OPPORTUNITY

*"Prosperity is an instrument
to be used, not a deity to be
worshipped."*
— *Calvin Coolidge*

The spark was probably lit in Haiti.

During all their voyaging and wandering, in the West Indies, the Caribbean, and South America, Jay Van Andel and Rich DeVos never overlooked anything that suggested an incentive for developing business. While covering one leg of their tropical island exploration, they had visited Haiti, where they were impressed by the diligence and skill of local craftsmen. Near Port-au-Prince, they discovered unique bowls, dishes, utensils, and curios of handcarved mahogany. Once they had returned to the States, it was relatively easy to obtain additional samples of native handicraft and arrange to import the objects they thought would be most marketable in department stores and other retail outlets in western Michigan.

It was at this period in their lives that they cemented their partnership by giving it a trade name: Ja-Ri Corporation. At first glance, Van Andel and DeVos seem unlikely partners for such a venture. Though both are friendly conversationalists, Van Andel tends to be reserved and somewhat introspective by comparison with DeVos, who has always been gregarious and outspoken. Their personalities are reflected in their hobbies and recreational pursuits.

Given a choice, Van Andel might choose to find his adventures in a novel while DeVos likes the stimulus of getting together with friends for more active pursuits and lively discussions.

Physically, there is no resemblance, with DeVos's medium build and dark hair a clear contrast to the taller, fair-haired Van Andel. Yet to focus on such superficial differences is to overlook an important business principle: The success of a partnership seldom demands similarities of temperament and bearing. Rather, it is nourished by mutually shared objectives and a common vision, factors that in this case certainly strengthened the relationship between the two partners.

Of equal value is the fact that the men share a similar heritage and style of upbringing. Both are the sons or grandsons of immigrants who migrated to America from Holland at the turn of the century. Both come from families that taught them as children to honor the old Dutch traditions of hard work and fine craftsmanship. And both have long since learned that good business sense depends first of all on an understanding and appreciation of sound economic values.

Despite prior experience with the aviation venture and a solid grasp of practical business concepts, Van Andel and DeVos faced questions that were tough to answer, most coming from the retailers who were their prospective customers.

"How long will it take to fill my orders?"
"How substantial is your inventory?"
"How reliable are your suppliers?"
"What promotions are you planning?"

They were quizzed about many other pertinent matters, such as advertising budgets, the terms of purchase or consignment, damaged merchandise and returns, and the size of the product line that would be available.

"We quickly discovered that starting a wholesale operation would require a sizable capital investment," Van Andel recalls. "We realized that we had not selected an easy way to go because we'd have to be lucky to find products so unique, so desirable that the whole world would come to us, rather than to some other better-known firm down the road."

Acknowledging that the products they envisioned, though attractive, did not fill the bill, they explored other avenues. "There *had* to be another way," says DeVos, "for people like us, who wanted a business of our own, to get started. Here we had a knack for sales and plenty of ambition, but we certainly didn't begin to have the capital resources needed to carve our niche in the precarious marketplace we now pictured."

The breakthrough came in 1949 from an unexpected quarter. On a visit from Chicago made expressly for the purpose, Van Andel's second cousin, Neal Maaskant, described a business venture that was earning him $1,000 a month. Jay Van Andel's interest was kindled to the point where he requested a second meeting so that DeVos could also attend and learn the details.

The venture was built entirely on the direct selling of the food supplement developed by Nutrilite Products, Inc. A food supplement appealed to the two partners as a product that was unique and that could build a demand. In essence, it was a blend of alfalfa, parsley, watercress, yeast, minerals, and vitamins that had been formulated in 1933 by Carl Rehnborg, a chemist and health food devotee. After studying diet deficiencies in China and observing that many

Americans lost nutrients through overcooking food and improper eating habits, Rehnborg had created a supplement that would provide a better, more healthful balance.

The best part about the sales plan described by Maaskant was that it required only a modest initial investment, yet rewarded salespeople in two ways: (1) With a profit on each food supplement program that was sold, and (2) With a second profit in the form of a small bonus on the products that were sold by the distributors the salesperson recruited and trained.

"I talked with Rich about the Nutrilite plan after our meeting," recalls Jay Van Andel. "We recognized that we had no experience in direct selling — we hadn't even known what the term meant. But, since we definitely were not interested in the retail store type of business, direct selling showed more promise. It was a means of getting quickly and easily into a business that would start producing income soon.

"So I said, 'You know, I think this guy's got something to offer and we should really get with it.'"

Their next step — attending a Chicago sales presentation, where they met the company's president — clinched their decision. They came out of the meeting convinced that the product and plan would sell in western Michigan.

"We started out much like Amway distributors do today," says DeVos. "We paid $49 for a sales kit, two boxes of Nutrilite Double X, and some literature. Then we went out and tried our hand at selling the product and recruiting distributors into the business."

FROM HUMBLE BEGINNINGS: OPPOSITE, *founding father of Nutrilite Products, Inc., Dr. Carl Rehnborg.* ABOVE, *key Nutrilite agents Van Andel and DeVos look on as Nutrilite distributor Pauline Saltzman receives the grand prize of a new Hillman Minx sedan in 1956 "Your Nutrilite Radio Theatre" story contest.* BELOW, LEFT, *Ja-Ri Corporation offices in 1950.* BELOW, RIGHT, *Nutrilite's Buena Park, California, office complex today.*

What motivated Van Andel and DeVos in the Nutrilite program were the same persuasions that today impress prospects about the Amway plan: the option to elect either a part- or full-time venture; a start-up cost almost anyone could afford; and products people believe in. As the two partners learned from Maaskant, a basic concept of the marketing plan was that distributors first had to become enthusiastic about the product by using it themselves, then sell it, and reach into the pool of satisfied customers to find sales recruits.

"The product did require quite a bit of selling," explains Van Andel. "The typical presentation took at least 45 minutes and demanded a fair degree of persuasion and skill." Displaying that skill and more, the partners were soon building an impressive force of customers and distributors. During 1950, their first full year with Nutrilite, they grossed some $82,000, a sum that more than quadrupled the following year.

A company bulletin praised Van Andel and DeVos as "idea men," models of success because they followed through on their ideas, "living proof that free enterprise is still possible in America." Projected sales for 1952 were half a million dollars.

The two partners had now reached a plateau where they had to commit less of their time to selling products and more to building a distributor network. A first step was to travel to other towns, where they placed ads in the local newspapers introducing the Nutrilite sales opportunity and announcing get-acquainted meetings. This procedure usually gained at least one new distributor, although sometimes the results were less rewarding. DeVos laughs about the night they ambitiously scheduled a meeting in a hall with a capacity of two hundred — and attracted only *two* attendees. Nevertheless, with characteristic good humor and persistence, the partners gave their sales pitch. It was during this stage of development that they also bought a former supermarket building on Franklin Street in Grand Rapids and transformed it into a spartan office and training headquarters.

These were the years when Van Andel and DeVos perfected the sales concepts and policies on which Amway Corporation would later be founded. They split their responsibilities in line with their respective skills. Van Andel, the writer, produced informative sales presentations for their distributors, detailing all the steps necessary to a successful sale. DeVos, the motivator, inspired and trained the sales force. With a talent for reaching people and kindling enthusiasm, he could command immediate confidence in the goals and principles he presented. Both men shared one important quality: an inborn sense of leadership. Through hard work, long hours, and the constant establishment of new goals, they set a pace that inspired distributors to follow their example and get results.

AMWAY: THE EARLY YEARS

These were the events and principles that later made it possible for Van Andel and DeVos to launch Amway so quickly and successfully, in contrast to the faltering steps that characterize the progress of most new companies. Yet not even its founders expected Amway to take off so well. "I'm still overwhelmed by the initial rapid growth," insists DeVos. "We started out just to build a business, hoping we'd survive and earn a reasonable income. Then the business just sort of took off. The idea caught on and before we knew it we were really hanging on to a rocket."

As mentioned earlier, the new Amway Corporation grossed half a million dollars during 1960, its first full year of operation. But the "rocket" DeVos talked about was already going into orbit. Sales doubled each year for the next two years and by 1963 had reached *twelve times* the 1960 level.

EMBRYONIC YEARS: The outward look and inner workings of Amway in the early 1960s.

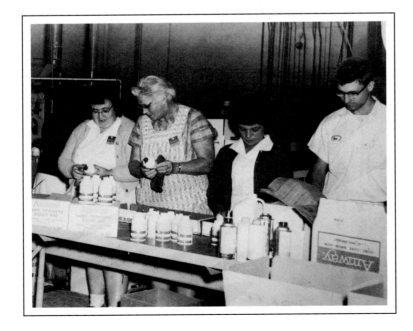

OFF AND RUNNING: ABOVE, headquarters of a young company experiencing spectacular growth, circa 1963. BELOW, early days on the aerosol production line.

In response to this accelerating growth, the company had started modest manufacturing operations on its own to solve some of the product supply demands. One of the first production employees, Bob Rooker, recalls, "When I came to work full time in the spring of 1962 when the company began its own aerosol manufacturing, we had 12 employees. By fall we had well over 50."

At the same time, in answer to increasing requests from distributors for speedier availability of products, a semitrailer truck was acquired to make regular deliveries to regional warehouses. By the end of 1963, the fleet had multiplied to 16. During the same period, the employee roster at the home office escalated from 84 to almost 300. The growth of the physical plant was further evidence of the company's overall success. Modest additions to the original service station were followed by the completion of an Executive Office Building in May 1962. A contemporary *Amagram*

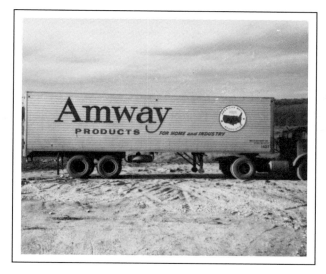

HANGING ON TO A ROCKET: TOP, Amway steps into the "Space Age" with the completion of a modern new Executive Office Building in 1965. BOTTOM LEFT, Amway's first semitrailer truck, dawn of the great Amway truck fleet. BOTTOM RIGHT, the marquee of the old Grand Rapids Civic Auditorium trumpets 1962's Distributor Convention, whose attendance levels doubled the previous year's total.

magazine article described the new building as "the hub of Amway, with glass-enclosed tunnels connecting present plant and future buildings in true Space-Age fashion."

Kay Evans remembers well the day the building was opened. An "Open House" had been planned to coincide with Amway's annual meeting in Grand Rapids. But, as is often the case, the week beforehand was a hectic period, with contractors pushing to complete the finishing touches and employees pitching in to help get everything ready. "I must have been quite a sight," says Evans, "caught in the act of hosing down floors and setting up tables of coffee and cookies as our visiting distributors literally peered through the windows to sneak a glimpse of what this new place was really like."

Although it would be several weeks before the permanent staff could move in, the company already had plans for another new building, this one for printing and shipping. It, too, would be connected by glass corridors. "We always seemed to be playing catch-up," says Rooker. "We'd expand and by the time the addition was completed, we'd be ready to expand again. We never seemed to achieve that comfortable state of having enough space, enough equipment, and enough time."

He was hardly exaggerating. In its first seven years alone, Amway had to complete 45 plant expansions just to keep pace with the company's spectacular growth. By 1984 there had been over 80 major building projects.

It was auspicious that 600 distributors showed up for the convention that spring of 1962, more than double the number that had attended the first assembly on home territory the year before. Held in the large Grand Rapids Civic Auditorium, the convention not only provided new information on the Amway sales plan and commercial sales, but included

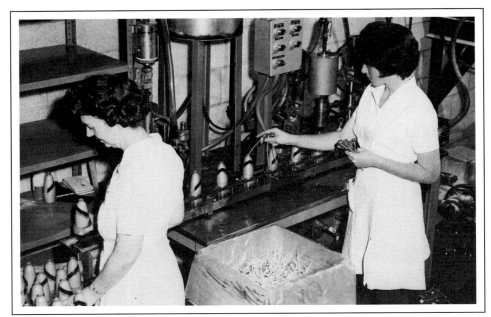

DECADE OF DEVELOPMENT: TOP LEFT, Amway's Del Remme meets the press to air the merits of S-A-8 Laundry Compound. TOP RIGHT, Clair Knox displays award received upon his retirement in 1983 after two decades of distinguished service as consultant to Amway Corporation. BOTTOM, aerosol production in 1965 — one more area of skyrocketing growth.

training sessions on new products. Among them were Amway's stainless steel cookware line, water conditioners, home-care products, and a battery additive called Vitalyte.

To coordinate this kind of growth and assure greater administrative efficiency, the major divisions — Sales, Services, and Manufacturing — were merged into a single Amway Corporation, effective January 1, 1964. "Because he was older," jokes DeVos, "Van Andel was named chairman, while I became the president." Under this reorganization the new corporation had seven divisions to cover the respective responsibilities of manufacturing, sales, marketing, operations, finance, legal, and personnel.

The chairman and president then retained the services of a direct-sales consultant and specialist, Clair Knox, a friend from their Nutrilite experience. He was made responsible for ensuring that productive systems and methods were followed; that appropriate managers were recruited, both from inside and outside the company; and that plans for the future were constantly reviewed and evaluated. In 1983, having served in this capacity for more than two decades, he offered this tribute to the two leaders and their wives: "Rich and Helen DeVos and Jay and Betty Van Andel have worked diligently at making successful the most outstanding and most rewarding partnership of this century."

THE FIVE-YEAR MILESTONE

By 1964, barely five years after the founding of Amway in Ada, Michigan, the young corporation was reaping the rewards of diligence, dedication, and continuing hard work. By year's end, the personnel department was hiring the 500th employee; the sales division had reached the $10 million mark; and marketing was offering 32 new products, including aerosol lotions, fabric softeners, iron-on patches, and moth crystals, all of which had undergone the most thorough research and testing before being approved for production.

An end-of-year issue of *Amagram* magazine dubbed 1964 "The Year of the Big Grow," noting that distributor ranks had swelled from 30,000 to more than 65,000 and that 8,000 new distributors were being recruited each month.

Many economic conditions outside the company had also contributed to the year's astonishing record. Consumer spending multiplied; the average disposable income was on the rise; and the ranks of distributors were boosted by an increasing number of women looking for jobs, both to achieve more independence and supplement the family income. Another factor was the combination of greater automobile production and lagging highway construction. The resultant traffic jams, especially in the days before shopping malls became so commonplace, resulted in a favorable climate for shoppers who preferred the convenience of having products delivered right to their doorsteps.

Amway began stepping up support for its growing army of distributors. For one thing, the company conducted monthly, expense-paid seminars at the headquarters in Ada, for those achieving the title of Direct Distributor, the level at which their sales record qualified them to deal directly with Amway. Besides motivating distributors to increase their sales in order to qualify, these seminars aimed at a dual objective: to give people in the field a stronger sense of identity with the home office and to give management an opportunity to reinforce the commitments of its distributors.

YEAR OF THE BIG GROW: ABOVE, Chairman Van Andel and President DeVos of the newly reorganized Amway Corporation. BELOW, former President (then Congressman) Gerald R. Ford addresses the 1964 Distributor Convention in Grand Rapids.

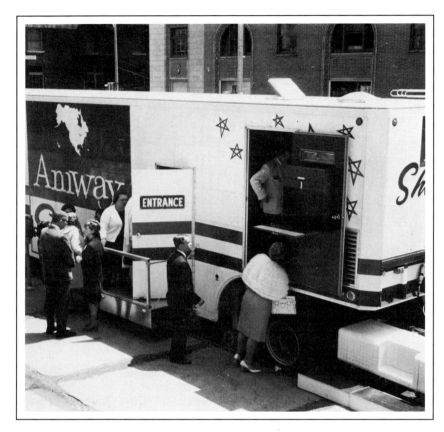

ON A ROLL: *ABOVE, a second-generation Showcase bus took to the roads in 1965 at a cost of some $75,000. BELOW, in 1963 the first Showcase bus, sign of increasing support for the growing distributor network, began putting Amway's products on the map from coast to coast.*

Road shows also provided dramatic support and produced demonstrable results. The "Showcase" bus was a case in point, a big hit and always booked solid for many months in advance. Completely stocked with Amway products and literature, the bus first took to the road in 1963 to visit the communities of active distributors. Its purpose was to present the company's products to prospective customers, as well as to serve as a recruitment vehicle for new distributors. Advance publicity assured record turnouts as the Showcase verified Amway's presence in communities from coast to coast.

The mid-1960s also saw a sequence of events and situations that, while at first seemingly unrelated, proved to be highly advantageous to one of Amway's major selling efforts. The subjects: environmental quality and water pollution. Americans everywhere were becoming concerned about the ecology and the increasing threat of water pollution. Newspapers, magazines, and television broadcasts particularly focused their attention on white foam bubbling along rivers or ringing the smudged shorelines of ponds and lakes. Commentators described America's inland waters as giant "rinse-tubs" clogged with washday residues. The villains in this case were detergents.

Consumers became familiar with the tongue-twisting term "biodegradable," as they were told about new types of detergents being researched that would be compatible with nature and would break down quickly without harming the sensitive ecosystems of lakes and streams.

The only hitch was that, according to experts who testified before Congress, it would be several years before these "safe" cleaning products could be readied and marketed. Taking issue with the experts, and seizing the opportunity to bring credit to Amway detergents, Amway called national attention to an already well-documented fact: Amway's L.O.C. Liquid Organic Cleaner and S-A-8™ Laundry Detergent were both biodegradable. Congressional testimony notwithstanding, they were readily obtainable from Amway distributors anywhere in the country.

Amway was the first to offer nationally marketed biodegradable detergents to the consumer.

REACHING NEW ORBITS

It was inevitable that Amway would rocket northward into Canada, as well as blazing new trails east, west, and south. The event took place officially in 1962 when Amway "went international" by establishing Amway of Canada, Ltd. Prior to this, distributors in the Detroit area had requested approval to extend their operations across the border, where more and more Canadians were asking how and where they could purchase Amway products. The move got under way slowly, but by 1966 the fledgling Canadian operation was contributing more than $2 million to the company's total sales of $38 million.

IT'S AMWAY, NATURALLY: Rich DeVos takes to the airwaves to spread the word on L.O.C. and S-A-8, America's first nationally marketed biodegradable detergents.

New business on both sides of the border was continuously straining Amway's production and distribution facilities, necessitating constant construction, often at a frantic pace. A combination warehouse and liquid products building, completed in the middle of the decade and hailed as "the first of the big ones," had to be supplanted merely a year later by one more than twice its size. To help ship products to regional warehouses, now 28 and still growing, the company constructed a railway spur to the Grand Trunk Railroad line. Two miles long, it was informally christened the Amway Railroad after Van Andel and DeVos drove gold-colored spikes and dedicated the spur to "the thousands of men and women who make the Amway opportunity work."

A key management decision resulted in the creation of a separate division devoted to product research and development. Of special interest was a distributor test center, established in Fort Wayne, Indiana, to experiment with new marketing ideas and procedures. Recognizing the basic importance of sales presentations, management also ordered two new color offset presses for the printing plant and a new sound studio for audio and audio-visual programs.

Following the success of the initial Showcase bus, a second one was outfitted at a cost of some $75,000, a gleaming white tractor-trailer emblazoned with the Amway emblem and laden with literature and samples of the growing family of products. The new Showcase was introduced in May 1965 during the Fifth International Convention in Grand Rapids.

"Because few distributors have the opportunity to visit us in Ada," said Van Andel to five thousand enthusiastic distributors at the convention, "we're taking the plant to them. Distributors can use the Showcase to stimulate their sales meetings and show the Amway opportunity to new customers and distributors." In another effort to increase the awareness of Amway products in widespread communities, he and DeVos announced that the company would be sponsoring ABC Radio's Saturday news broadcast by the popular commentator Paul Harvey.

WORKING ON THE RAILROAD: Amway's owners drive a gold spike to signal the completion of the 10,000-foot Amway railroad spur into Ada.

GOING INTERNATIONAL: Amway's first international office, opened in Canada in 1962.

WELCOME ABOARD: Rich DeVos greets Paul Harvey (to his right) as the popular broadcaster visits Ada to mark Amway's sponsorship of his Saturday news program.

SOURCES OF PRIDE: *TOP RIGHT, 13 loyal employees receive Amway's first five-year pins, in 1966. BOTTOM LEFT, 1968's Distributor Convention in Grand Rapids attracts record attendance — and enthusiasm. BOTTOM RIGHT, page from an early Personal Shoppers Catalog, a "dream book in living color."*

These were just a few of numerous media efforts increasingly lending support to the selling efforts in the field. But these communications programs were not undertaken without placing a considerable work load on the people in the home office. "Even with the addition of college and high-school student help," reported a 1966 *Amagram* magazine, "packaging and production could not keep up with the demand. A call went out for volunteer workers from other departments to help out in the emergency and many office workers appeared on the lines every morning at six o'clock to keep the orders moving to the distributors in the field."

By mid-1967, hiring had raised plant staff levels to more than 700 full-time employees. Sales that year hit $50 million and were to rise another 30 percent during the next twelve months. With more than 150 regular items already in its product line, Amway made a major new product commitment with the introduction of Artistry® Cosmetics. Another innovation was the creation of the Personal Shoppers® Service Catalog, designed to meet buying trends, which were reflecting strong consumer interest in ordering products at home.

Amway declared 1968 "The Year of the Distributor," planning and sponsoring special programs nationwide, climaxed by the annual convention. Governors, senators, and other state and local dignitaries attended the commemorative ceremonies in the Grand Rapids Civic Auditorium, which was packed to capacity with distributors who had chartered buses and planes to make sure they did not miss this noteworthy event.

"YEAR OF ACHIEVEMENT"

That was the designation for 1969, Amway's Tenth Anniversary Year, when goals were set and achieved again and again. By this time, there were more than 100,000 distributors throughout the United States and in parts of Canada. Enthusiastically applying the slogan "A Sale A Day," and with a line of almost 200 products to offer customers, the company grossed $85 million in twelve months. North of the border, Amway's spreading influence led to the appointment of a translator to translate sales and training literature for the increasing ranks of French-speaking distributors in Canada.

Yet, as had been the case since the very origins of the Amway concept of selling, the physical provisions, the training capabilities, the product lines — all these were secondary to the less tangible *personal magic* that achieved sales records and inspired others to greater and greater accomplishments. Among the names of distributor couples who set the pace during this significant period in Amway history were Art and Ollie Charlton, Jere and Eileen Dutt, and Charlie and Elsie Marsh. They had made history by becoming Double Diamond Direct Distributors the year before.

MAKING HISTORY: ABOVE, TOP, George Romney, then governor of Michigan, addresses the 1966 Distributor Convention in Grand Rapids. ABOVE, BOTTOM, DeVos and Van Andel cut a cake in celebration of the tenth birthday of their thriving young enterprise. LEFT, A young Wally Buttrick lends a hand at the printing presses.

Then, in 1969, the Marshes became the first couple to attain the Triple Diamond level of achievement.

How did these couples manage to set such remarkable sales records?

The story of Art and Ollie Charlton, formerly of Massachusetts and now living in Florida, is a dramatic example. Within six years of signing up with Amway they had achieved the level of Crown Direct Distributor and were going strong. Before then, they had already tried two other "independent" ventures. The first had been a fuel-oil business in Massachusetts, which had been reasonably successful. But the second had been an ice cream franchise in Phoenix, Arizona, where they moved as part of a "retirement" plan. After watching their life savings dwindle as the business faltered, they sold out and moved back to Massachusetts.

Fortunately, they had just learned about Amway and had decided, since the investment was negligible, to give it a try. "We tried Amway products ourselves and were really impressed," Art recalls. "We began our business with a burning desire to be successful and we didn't care how many hours we put in or how much effort it took. Within three months we were Direct Distributors and by the end of the first year we were making more money than we had ever made before."

Part of the excitement and reward of the new business was, for them, the realization that they were bringing other distributors into the business and watching them succeed in the same way they had done. "We were enjoying what we were doing so much," Ollie recalls, "that we had not the slightest urge to slow down and take it easy. We loved it — and we still love it. We've seen so many people, just like we were, who wanted so badly to succeed and did it by pure determination and hard work. It's the most exciting thing in the world to see those people break through."

One of the factors that helped the Charltons to reach out to others and communicate so well was that they had been through the mill themselves and had learned what it was like to invest savings in a shaky venture and have to quit.

THE MANY FACES OF AMWAY: ABOVE, Executive Committee Meeting, 1967. TOP RIGHT, Charlie and Elsie Marsh, first couple to reach Triple Diamond, are greeted by Rich DeVos in Ada on their Diamond Day. BOTTOM RIGHT, employees and facilities keep pace with Amway's phenomenal growth as the company moves into the 1970s.

YEAR OF THE GREAT DISASTER: The aerosol plant and all its contents burn to the ground on July 18, 1969.

Part of their reward has been security, of course. Yet in addition to the obvious trappings of financial success, they receive the greatest satisfaction from being able to share the Amway opportunity. "Amway is our way of life," they agree, "and as long as the opportunity exists to help others help themselves, we'll be right there doing our bit."

Amway's tenth anniversary was also known as "The Year of the Great Disaster." It had been a period of heavy construction to keep pace with increasing demands, including numerous additions to the plant and the completion of a modern 150,000-square-foot warehouse. Physically, Amway was in a state of great good health and growing stronger every day.

Then came July 18, 1969.

Jay Van Andel was at his home in Ada. Rich DeVos was vacationing aboard his sailboat, moored off Charlevoix, Michigan. "At 6:30 A.M.," DeVos recalls, "a cousin of mine who is also a boat enthusiast came over and pounded on my cabin and got me out of my bunk.

"'Do you realize that your factory burned down last night?' he asked me hoarsely.

"I was almost in a state of shock. No one had been able to reach me. Or they were too busy trying to cope with the problems at hand to worry where I might be. I called right away and arranged for the company plane to pick me up."

While en route to Ada, DeVos was able to piece the story together. News reports indicated that an explosion had occurred shortly after 11:00 the previous night in the aerosol building, followed by a flash fire. For a time, it had been feared that some employees might be trapped inside the plant. Fortunately, by 3 A.M., Van Andel, who had reached the scene shortly after the first explosion, was able to report that there were no fatalities. However, several employees had received serious burns and had been taken immediately to the University of Michigan Burn Center for emergency treatment.

Although losses were initially estimated as high as $700,000, they might have been much greater, according to Grand Rapids Fire Chief Robert Veit, had not the company's fire control installations done their job. Noting that the sprinklers had contained the fire in the aerosol plant, he called the system "a credit to company planning."

Catastrophic though the fire was, it served as a catalyst to bring Amway people together in a unique and dedicated effort to get the company back on its feet with as little disruption as possible. "Jay Van Andel worked through the night," recalls Kay Evans, "in left field, right field, center field," coordinating efforts to salvage vital records from surrounding offices that might be imperiled. At the same time, he tried to cope with journalists, broadcasters, and other media people who showed up and wanted to be briefed on what had happened and what plans the company had for recovery.

They might best have stuck around to see for themselves. "We had a meeting the first thing next morning," says Evans in discussing the company's speedy marshalling of its forces for recovery. "I don't even remember where, but Jay told us to get in touch with the staff and at 8 A.M. we held our first discussion."

The immediate, unanimous decision was to rebuild, and as quickly as possible. Even as investigators sifted through the debris, unsuccessfully attempting to isolate the cause of the blaze that had destroyed the old plant, work pressed forward on the new one. One of the first matters of business was to arrange for supplies of replacement products through a contractor in Holland, Michigan. At the same time, the latest in new equipment was ordered and just six months later an official memorandum announced that "the aerosol plant has been completely reconstructed, one of the most modern and efficient such plants in the nation. Its mixing areas, filling lines, and gassing section are all located in different adjacent buildings to divide any hazard."

This triumphant recovery, documenting Amway's unique style of teamwork and coordination, was a fitting — if quite unexpected — closing to the first decade.

FROM OUT OF THE ASHES: ABOVE, *attempts to contain the blaze.* BELOW, *on "Appreciation Day," Rich DeVos and Amway Corporation thank Grand Rapids' firefighters for their efforts.*

The keys to achievement in an Amway business: goals, effort, and commitment.

Chapter Four

TO RUN WHILE OTHERS WALK

"First, say to yourself what you would be; and then do what you have to do."
— *Epictetus*

"What are some of your dreams?" asks the Amway brochure. "A new home? A new car? A college or private education for your children? Travel?"

For many people, such dreams are as unstable as shifting sands. For Amway distributors, however, visions of material success and financial security lie on the bedrock of the Sales and Marketing Plan. Described as "one of the finest examples of free enterprise on the current business scene," the Plan offers "a working opportunity to invest your time, your effort, and your energy for profit ... without financial risk." One of the remarkable ingredients is its adaptability. Individuals from all walks of life and in more than 40 countries and territories around the world successfully follow the same course of action.

Amway's extensive line of products is divided into specific product groups, or "businesses." In the United States, for example, there are seven businesses: Home Care, Personal Care, Health & Fitness, Home Tech, Catalog, Commercial, and Services. Such programs as long-distance phone service and a travel reservation service comprise Services, the newest Amway business. Other markets have some or all of these businesses.

Distributors earn money by selling products to customers who, in turn, often recommend other potential customers. It is suggested that appointments with prospects be made beforehand, rather than calling on them unexpectedly. "We don't do cold canvassing," explains DeVos. "Instead, it's what I call 'back-fence selling.'"

Distributors profit in direct proportion to their sales efforts. The Sales and Marketing Plan, according to Amway literature, "can provide whatever you want it to provide, a supplementary income of a few dollars a week or a far-flung business of your own which is nationwide, even international, in scope. *It's up to you!*"

The concept of the Plan traces its roots back to Nutrilite. Distributors were recruited, each entitled to buy products at a basic discount. Distributors also received monthly bonuses, depending on sales volume, and were qualified to become "sponsors" after they began servicing a minimum of 25 regular customers. "Sponsoring" then and now is defined as bringing other individuals into the business by persuading them that they, too, can profit through the sale of products and later by becoming sponsors themselves. Distributors receive no immediate income from recruiting, but later are entitled to receive bonuses from the company in direct proportion to the business developed by them and the people they have sponsored.

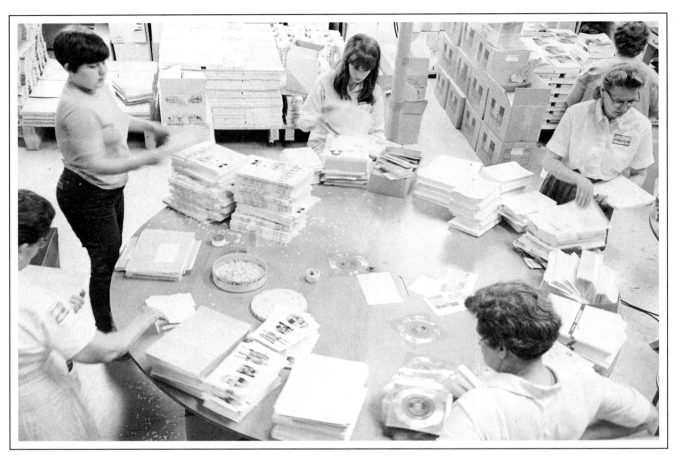

SPREADING THE WORD: Assembling early product and motivational literature.

The Nutrilite plan offered a modest variety of product literature and some fundamental sales aids. Guidelines were provided for holding motivational meetings, both to inspire current distributors and recruit newcomers. To these basic materials, Van Andel and DeVos added many of their own inventive touches, designed to motivate prospects more quickly and effectively. At weekly sales meetings, for example, they would pass out postcards for distributors to address and sign. The cards advertised certain products and requested that the distributor be given an opportunity to show them and demonstrate their advantages. Follow-up contacts and visits often resulted in product sales and sometimes in the subsequent recruitment of new distributors.

The motivational meetings were symbolic of the talents and skills the two partners contributed to the selling and marketing activities. Van Andel, with a flair for creativity, wrote scripts and staged skits that added color and inspiration to these occasions. DeVos, with a relish for the spoken word, added his oratorical skills to motivate audiences.

Other innovations were constantly introduced as Amway's business grew and distributors began achieving higher and higher levels of sales and sponsorships. At the core of the business is the Amway Sales Kit received by every new distributor. It contains literature about Amway, selling the products, and presenting the Plan. The optional Product Kit contains a representative sampling of best-selling products that are in constant demand and that can be easily and efficiently demonstrated to consumers. Two points, among others, are emphasized: The products are the most effective on the market; and there is a money-back guarantee on every product bearing the Amway name.

With the help of the two kits, plus training and encouragement by an active and enthusiastic sponsor, the new distributor is well-equipped and motivated to go out and sell. The necessary supplies of Amway products are obtained through sponsors or through the Direct Distributors heading each group. There is a considerable amount of flexibility built into the Plan, since distributors sell products at prices they establish.

The "gross profit" (the difference between the purchase price and the selling price) can thus vary from distributor to distributor for any given quantity and type of product. It provides immediate income, however, and increases with the number of retail customers and sales.

NEW INCENTIVES, HIGHER ACHIEVEMENTS

"The buck doesn't stop there," to paraphrase President Truman's famous comment. This immediate income is but the first step on the path to earnings that can be substantial. Distributors can look forward to other incentives. One is the Performance Bonus, based on Point Value (PV) and Business Volume (BV). Each Amway product has an assigned PV, with points accumulated through the sales of the product. BV is the dollar value of the products a distributor purchases, whether sold to retail customers, purchased for his own sponsored distributors, or used by himself. Distributors who achieve a total PV of between 100 and 299 in one month earn 3 percent of their BV — and the higher the monthly PV, the greater the bonus percentage of BV earned. The maximum bonus — 25 percent — is achieved by generating at least 7,500 points.

Distributors can increase their Performance Bonus in two ways: by increasing the number of retail sales, or by sponsoring new distributors who make sales at retail. Since the Performance Bonus is calculated not only on the distributor's own PV and BV, but on those of the distributors sponsored, there is an incentive to expand the business through a combination of retail selling and sponsoring, and then by encouraging others down the line to follow suit.

As can be clearly seen, individual business growth in turn triggers ever-greater rewards. A distributor achieves the level of Direct Distributor (DD) when his total Point Value (including the accumulated PVs for those in his group) reaches 7,500 for three consecutive months. Direct Distributors have the privilege of buying their products direct from Amway Corporation, through one of the company's distribution centers. They also receive bonuses for distributors they have sponsored who also achieve Direct, with the monetary amount equaling three percent of the new DD's monthly group business volume.

SHOW AND TELL: ABOVE, the "Economic Tree of Life," once located in Amway's Center of Free Enterprise, offers graphic demonstration of the fruits of human labor. BELOW, Rich DeVos lets visual aids help tell the story in one of his many inspiring distributor talks of the 1960s.

A familiar term among Amway people is "drawing the circles." This simply refers to the graphic method used by many distributors at recruitment meetings to demonstrate on a chalkboard the ever-widening circles of distributors that make up a group and increase the eventual income. If it all looks rather impersonal on a chalkboard, it is anything but that in real life. Dallas and Betty Beaird, Crown Ambassador Direct Distributors from California who have been distributors since 1965, can attest to the fellowship inherent in this strategy. "Amway takes time and effort," they counsel, "but we have enjoyed working together, sharing the business opportunity with friends and family, and making new friends at meetings, conventions, and on trips. It has made it possible for us to help others in many ways. Our business has been built on friendship, and we look forward to sharing with others the many opportunities and blessings we have experienced since coming into Amway."

As the number of Direct Distributors multiplied, sales volumes climbed, and sponsorship levels continued to radiate, Amway's motivational opportunities required periodic updating. One example of this was the creation of Personal Sales Award plaques and pins to reward consistency and achievement. The first such recognition comes in the form of what has become known as the "Believer's Pin," awarded for $100 worth of retail sales in one month. Small though it seems later, it is often cherished as a person's first realization that Amway is going to continue to recognize one's determination to succeed, all the way up the ladder.

Here are the basic award levels for Amway distributors. When a Distributor builds his business to a specified level, he becomes a Direct Distributor — an important Amway milestone. A Direct Distributor buys products, literature, and sales aids directly from Amway rather than from a sponsor or Direct Distributor. A distributor can advance to higher award levels — Crown Ambassador being the highest — by continuing to build his business.

CROWN AMBASSADOR DIRECT DISTRIBUTOR
CROWN DIRECT DISTRIBUTOR
TRIPLE DIAMOND DIRECT DISTRIBUTOR
DOUBLE DIAMOND DIRECT DISTRIBUTOR
EXECUTIVE DIAMOND DIRECT DISTRIBUTOR
DIAMOND DIRECT DISTRIBUTOR
EMERALD DIRECT DISTRIBUTOR
PEARL DIRECT DISTRIBUTOR
RUBY DIRECT DISTRIBUTOR
PROFIT SHARING DIRECT DISTRIBUTOR
DIRECT DISTRIBUTOR
DISTRIBUTOR

What could be more symbolic of accomplishment than fine jewels? Early in its development, Amway set the pace for achievement by recognizing each level of accomplishment with the name of a precious stone. The first, in 1962, was the Ruby, followed in succession by Pearl, Emerald, and Diamond. As sales volumes and sponsorships exceeded all expectations, there were no stones available for use which were commonly considered more precious than diamonds. The solution was to specify a Double Diamond (established in 1966) for the next higher level and then the Triple Diamond (in 1969.) Further accomplishments resulted in the designation of the first Crown award in 1970 and finally, seven years later, the Crown Ambassador, the highest pinnacle to which an Amway distributor can aspire.

The first to attain the Ruby level were Jere Dutt and his late wife, Eileen, of Ohio. The first Crowns were Charlie and Elsie Marsh of Florida. Breaking the sound barrier into Crown Ambassador were Dick Marks and his late wife, Bunny, in 1977, followed closely by the Marshes, Chuck and Jean Strehli of Texas, and Jerry and Sharyn Webb, also of Texas.

The Markses characterize the kind of involvement that makes it possible to achieve these high goals and still enjoy family life and a wonderful life-style. They were struggling to pay the bills, he as a Winnipeg, Manitoba, policeman and she as a secretary, when they first decided to try Amway. "After a year and a half part time and three years full time," recalls Dick, "we had total financial freedom. We could live in the city of our choice, buy the home of our choice, have the cars of our choice ...."

Dick and Bunny were Emeralds when they decided to move to Minneapolis and spend full time on Amway. Deciding to make a real go of it, they rose to the Crown level in just two years. "Every year we said it can't get better," Bunny reminisced, "but it always did. We'd only been in the business six months when Dick told me I was too valuable to do housework. I always knew he was intelligent, but I realized he was getting smarter every day. And so I had a lady come in one day a week, then two days, and then Dick saw me moving her luggage in. I literally haven't cooked or ironed for 16 years. Talk about rewards!"

As has been the case with so many successful distributors, the Markses' success motivated their children (three of them, plus a son-in-law) to join forces as Amway distributors, keeping the business in the family and making it more enjoyable than ever.

As the incentive plans have been enhanced over the years, the degree of motivation and involvement has been substantially strengthened throughout the Amway ranks. Van Andel and DeVos have continually reminded their people that self-motivation must come first before any real achievement can be expected. Distributors are urged to set sales goals, to be clear about their sponsorship objectives, and to follow the steps that have been carefully formulated in the Sales and Marketing Plan.

CLIMBING THE LADDER: Jere and Eileen Dutt, first to reach the Ruby level, went on to become Amway's first Double Diamond Distributors.

KEEPING IN TOUCH

In 1975, emphasizing that distributors can achieve success if properly motivated, Amway promoted the simple, straightforward message, "Run while others walk!" It summed up the whole philosophy that there are no barriers standing in the way of those who *want* to succeed and that even the worst of times can be the best of times for building an Amway business.

Perhaps no one knows this better than Joe and Helyne Victor of Ohio, who were pioneers in the Amway business a quarter of a century ago. Reaching the Crown level in 1980, Joe commented, "We just feel lucky that we stuck with it, because we remember those that quit. People coming into the business now have everything to work with. We only had one product in the beginning. Of course, the greatest thing about Amway has always been its willingness to move forward."

To help its growing family of distributors to "run" and keep pace with new Amway programs, the company has undertaken a continuing series of advertising campaigns, which first began building the Amway image and lending sales support in 1965. Among the first such measures were sponsorship of a Saturday ABC newscast and print ads in a number of family-oriented magazines, including *McCall's*, *House & Garden*, the *Saturday Evening Post*, and *Parents*.

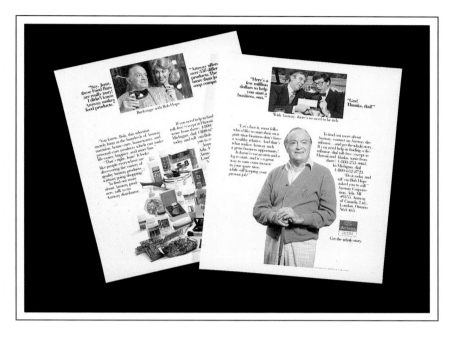

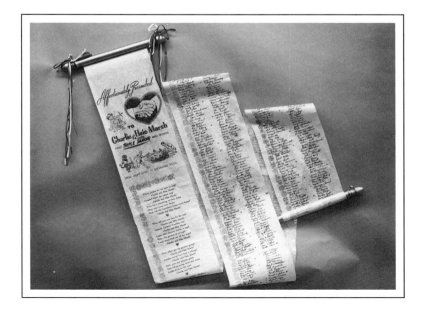

ROOM AT THE TOP: OPPOSITE, BOTTOM LEFT, Amway's co-founders take Joe and Helyne Victor on a special tour of the Ada complex on "Victor Day," November 20, 1974. OPPOSITE, TOP, 1965 Product and Sales Kit materials. OPPOSITE, CENTER, the Amway Distributor Crown Ambassador Pin. OPPOSITE, BOTTOM, the Amway Distributor Ruby Pin. ABOVE, TOP LEFT, samples of the early 1980s print ads that presented Bob Hope as Amway spokesman. ABOVE, TOP RIGHT, a series of 1968 Amway ads featuring illustrations by Norman Rockwell. ABOVE, BOTTOM LEFT, the range of distributor pin levels available in 1975. ABOVE, CENTER RIGHT, a 1969 Life magazine ad explains why "Amway is 'opportunity.'" BOTTOM RIGHT, the scroll of congratulatory signatures presented to new Triple Diamond Distributors Charlie and Elsie Marsh in 1969.

Today, Amway commercials reach millions of viewers and listeners over major TV and radio networks, while the products are seen in the pages of many of the nation's top-circulation magazines.

Communications are, and always have been, vital to Amway in reaching out with its message. Not all, however, have been fancy. In the early years of the company, many products were sold and people recruited through the aid of a simple little publication, *Amway News*, which Jay Van Andel wrote, mimeographed, and distributed. Amway encourages the continuation of this means of communication, with the result that many Direct Distributors publish their own newsletters and bulletins.

The best newsletters are those that not only provide useful information, but run brief, anecdotal case histories of success stories that motivate others. Some make a name for themselves with homespun philosophy, often quoted at recruitment meetings and rallies. Some examples:

- "Try and you may; don't and you won't."
- "Orders start a business; *repeat* orders keep it going."
- "If you wear out your shoes before the seat of your pants, you'll be more successful."
- "It is what we *think* we know that often prevents us from learning."
- "Be a leader; those who believe in following the crowd always end up in the rear."

Among the many kinds of internal communications that have proven successful are tape cassettes and videotapes, the more sophisticated offspring of earlier slide presentations and filmstrips. Van Andel and DeVos can be heard speaking on such pertinent subjects as "The Wishmores and the Havemores," "Freedom," "Ten Points that Make Amway Special," "Millionaire's Success Formula," "Try or Cry," "Now is the Time," "Today's Amway ... Better Than Ever," and "Excellence." Audio-visual cassettes feature such topics as "An Evening with Rich DeVos" and success stories by selected distributors. DeVos's selling tapes have sold over one million copies.

MOTIVATION MEDIA: OPPOSITE, TOP, the Amagram in 1971. OPPOSITE, CENTER, jacket of record album from the 1970 Amway Convention. OPPOSITE, BOTTOM, 1967 recording of Rich DeVos's inspirational "Selling America" speech. ABOVE, TOP, motivating the distributor, 1966. ABOVE, CENTER and BOTTOM, an assortment of books written by Rich DeVos and noted author Paul Conn to bring the Amway philosophy to thousands.

The two founders began long ago to strengthen the ever-vital artery of communications by keeping the dialogue flowing at all times. Realizing, however, that face-to-face communications are far more effective than tapes and other media that are less direct, they have taken all possible steps to emphasize the need for personal discussions. That was the reason behind the purchase of an island hotel and motorships — far more than using them as incentives.

"It's important in this business," says DeVos, "to keep in touch with people in the field. How do we make sure we keep listening to them? How do we create an atmosphere that makes it worth their time to come over and visit us? One way is to have a motorship or a resort hotel like Peter Island as a center for information-gathering and the productive exchange of ideas. One of management's most important functions is to spend time *listening*."

The home office in Ada, Michigan, is another center of attraction. Most corporate headquarters are places that have few attractions for anyone except the employees who work there. Not so at Amway. Distributors flow in steady streams into the Ada center, realistically and enthusiastically expecting that the red carpet will be out. New Direct Distributors are guests, at company expense, for two days of training seminars and meetings. Their names are added to the display board, as well as included, with photographs, in the current issue of *Amagram* magazine. Those who have reached higher levels of achievement are often pictured in front of homes, pools, cars, or other visible signs of success.

The hard edges of what we would normally associate with "business" meetings are softened by the family-like atmosphere that characterizes almost every Amway get-together, large or small. Newcomers are invited on stage to receive due recognition for their achievements, as well as to be introduced to and inspire their fellow distributors. Sharing experiences has long proven to be one of the best methods of encouraging camaraderie, as well as closer relationships that have time and again proven invaluable in times of personal sorrow or stress. This family-oriented tradition began in the early days of Amway when small gatherings were hosted at the homes of Betty Van Andel and Helen DeVos.

Astonishingly enough, that tradition does not get lost during training seminars attended by hundreds of distributors — or even during the annual conventions that now have become mammoth affairs, hosting people from many different nations.

The company stages rallies in many other locations, usually featuring special incentives and entertainment and sometimes guest speakers who are nationally known. For many years, some of the distributors themselves maintained a vocal group called the Sanborn Singers, one of the popular drawing cards of the annual convention. Distributors, too, hold rallies. Some rallies are small and local, but many are large regional events that attract thousands of participants.

Apart from the razzle-dazzle, the real purpose of rallies is to *communicate.* Furthermore, communication is invariably regarded as a two-way street; participants may listen to what others have to say, but they also express their own ideas.

Regardless of location, size, or sponsorship, Amway get-togethers are invariably charged with excitement. Success stories and inspirational messages are greeted with spontaneous clapping and cheering, as members of the audience respond with the conviction that they, too, can scale the heights of success with Amway.

"Ask a distributor what is the greatest reward in the business," comments Triple Diamond Direct Distributor Bill Campbell, "and you can almost tell how long that person has been in the business. The newest people always talk about income. By the time they've achieved any degree of success and length of service — and I'm talking months, not years — and you toss the same question at them, money is usually third, fourth, or fifth on the list."

The more important rewards he is referring to are likely to be the freedom that comes from owning a business, personal recognition, friendship, and the joys of sharing a commitment. As Campbell explains,

AN EXTENDED FAMILY: TOP, distributors pour through the lobby of a building in the Ada complex during the 1966 Amway Convention Tour. CENTER, the Sanborn Singers delight distributors at an annual convention. BOTTOM, Triple Diamond Direct Distributors Bill and Jan Campbell.

"You'll hear a couple say, 'We've found something we can work on together so we're not going off in different directions. It gives us a common purpose, a common goal — things we can talk about that we both understand.'"

Observers outside the business are always surprised to learn how many of the "newcomers" to Amway are in reality second-generation distributors, sharing the kind of commitment passed along to them by parents or other close relatives. As the company advances into its second quarter of a century, a healthy new brand of fellowship strengthens the ranks. These second-generation distributors are not the pioneers in the same sense as their predecessors, but people who have recognized the heritage that can be theirs, who are building their careers on the old traditions, but who also have the kinds of new life-styles they prefer.

Wally Buttrick of Michigan is a good example of this new generation. His initial exposure to Amway came in an unusual way. As a teenager, one of his *first* jobs was mowing lawns for Jay Van Andel. He became excited by the prospect of working for the new company and was an Amway employee for more than eight years. Then he made a decision.

"After all that exposure to this fantastic business," he says, "I decided to build my own Amway distributorship." Starting with a part-time business in a rented home, he moved through the Ruby and Emerald levels and then went on to achieve the Triple Diamond level. Although he is a full-time distributor, he takes time off to enjoy life. "The business has brought me many material things," says Wally, "but most of all I enjoy the freedom. My family and I are able to travel frequently. During my Amway career, I've been all across the United States, Canada, Australia, and the Caribbean.

"You have to set a goal and *really mean it*. Then believe you *can* achieve it and you will."

SCALING THE HEIGHTS: TOP, *Wally Buttrick, who made the transition from loyal employee to successful distributor, shares his unique Amway experiences at an early 1960s distributors meeting.* CENTER, *Rich DeVos and Jay Van Andel outside the Amway hangar in 1974.* BOTTOM, *spring 1974 aerial view of the Ada complex.*

TOP, (left to right) Nan, Jay, Steve, Betty, Dave, and Barb Van Andel. BOTTOM, (left to right) Dan, Cheri, Rich, Helen, Dave, and Dick DeVos.

Chapter Five

A FAMILY OF ACHIEVERS

*"On a team, there is no
substitute for confidence in
one's teammates."*
— Arthur Hays Sulzberger

One of Aesop's most popular fables relates the story of the various "Members of the Body," such as the Hands and the Teeth, who felt they were doing all the work while the Stomach just sat there and enjoyed all the food passed on down to it. So they decided to go on strike. The Fingers refused to pick up any food; the Mouth warned that it would remain closed; and the Throat asserted that it would not swallow anything.

This state of affairs continued for several days, with all the Members of the Body resolutely sustaining their strike against the Stomach. But pretty soon they discovered that the strike was affecting each of them. The Hands felt themselves growing feeble. The Mouth became parched and dry. Even the Legs complained that they were getting too weak to support the Members of the Body. So, as the wise Greek fabulist wrote, "They all discovered that even the Stomach, in its dull, quiet way, was performing very necessary functions and that all Members must work together or the Whole will go to pieces."

One of the words used most appropriately to describe the Amway concept of doing business is "supportive." Amway has aptly been described as "The World's Largest Family." Observers who may be deceived into thinking this is one of those pithy little promotional phrases coined by a public relations writer

are quickly reoriented when they find out what lies behind the spirit and philosophy of the company. There is almost no way to describe Amway other than as an enormous worldwide family.

This concept developed naturally and vigorously from the very beginning, through the personal beliefs and practices of the founders. Both Van Andel and DeVos have always been deeply religious Christians, traditionally taught to apply their faith to whatever they do in their lives and to voice their beliefs freely and unequivocally. As a dynamic and charismatic speaker, DeVos often declares to audiences that they are all "children of God," joined together in their attitudes and hopes. Yet he refrains from using Amway "to foist my private convictions on others" or "to use the Gospel to promote my business."

"Is Amway a Christian enterprise?"

When, on occasion, people have asked this question, Van Andel and DeVos have always explained it is not and that the Amway opportunity is open to *any* individual, regardless of faith. Furthermore, they have pointed out, "Businesses are not Christian or religious, people are." They affirm that "a business should be a reflection of its people, and it so happens that many of the Amway people, including us, believe there is a God in heaven who rules this world."

A FAMILY AFFAIR: The DeVos and Van Andel families with then Governor George Romney, at the 1967 Amway Distributors Convention. Top row, left to right: Betty Van Andel, Romney, Nan Van Andel, Jay Van Andel, Helen DeVos, Rich DeVos. Bottom row: Barb Van Andel, Cheri DeVos, Dan DeVos, Dick DeVos.

Rooted in their beliefs, Amway's founders have always been equally committed to their family bonds and traditions. "Parenthood," DeVos has often said, "cannot be delegated. Strong families are not made without strong people who believe enough in the value of parenthood to arrange their entire lives, if necessary, around home and family."

Helen DeVos and Betty Van Andel chose similar paths, devoting themselves to home and family, to civic improvement, to community cultural development, and to supporting their husbands' careers. Each has raised four children, guiding them along similar traditional roads of commitment and achievement.

It is not surprising, then, that the Amway philosophy reflects the belief of its originators in the vital significance of the family unit and family-oriented values. The concept of recruiting entire families as distributors evolved naturally and gradually from these origins until it became an integral part of the company's philosophy and even the Amway Sales and Marketing Plan itself. Married couples work together to achieve personal goals and share their duties and responsibilities. Oftentimes their children, who help their parents at first, later decide to become distributors themselves. Thus, it is not uncommon for entire families to be working together toward a common objective.

Conventions are always family-oriented. Invitations to seminars traditionally are extended to spouses, who share equally in all rewards and recognition for achievement, no matter which partner is the more active in the business.

"Family-oriented" is a many-faceted term. There are any number of distributors, for example, who are concerned about children who have *no* families, and who use part of their Amway income to rectify this unhappy state of affairs. Max and Marianne Schwarz are superb examples of this kind of outlook. Though they have achieved the status of Crown Ambassadors in West Germany, they dedicate every weekend to hosting two orphans, different children each week. Their long-range ambition is to build a home for orphans and handicapped children. "Through Amway," they say, "we hope to offer these children a more secure future."

THE SECRET IS PEOPLE

"The key to Amway is its people."

Ask someone who is close to the company and its organization to describe Amway and this is one of the themes that will be emphasized. The enthusiasm and esprit de corps of those who elect careers with Amway command universal recognition outside of the company as well as within. As one observer says about Amway's people, "They like who they are, they like what they are doing, they respect the company's owners, and they are considerate of each other."

BEHIND THE SCENES: TOP RIGHT: 1969 Amway employees meeting. CENTER RIGHT, office employees, 1965. BOTTOM RIGHT, early days on the powder line. BELOW, a 1960s research and development lab.

A quarter of a century ago, Jay Van Andel and Rich DeVos set the tone for their company's relationship with its people, and time has only strengthened their philosophy. "This business is more people-oriented than any other I know," says Van Andel. "We have millions of customers and over one million distributors. With that much involvement with people, it is important to understand them."

"Any understanding," adds his partner, "begins with respect. Only people make things happen. Only individuals drive nails to construct buildings. Only individuals drive trucks. Only individuals serve as doctors. That's how simple it is and that's why Amway works, because we respect and rely on individuals."

More than one million individuals, including over six thousand employees and one million independent distributors worldwide, have joined Amway in search of a better life. They remain because they find a spirit of togetherness, a sense of being part of the world's largest family. They have only to reflect on the families of the founders and the history of how they came together and stayed together, "blessed and privileged to do many great and exciting things."

DeVos is the first, however, to caution the members of this growing international family that they cannot take relationships for granted, whether between partners or between the company as a whole and its people. "These desirable relationships don't just coast along forever," he emphasizes. "They require work, care, forgiving, compromise, encouragement, time, and attention."

Communication is a critical element in maintaining strong relationships — one of the reasons employees are encouraged to attend regular "Speak-Up" sessions, during which they can exchange ideas and register opinions, pro and con, on issues at hand. The benefits of well-cemented relationships are many, to the company and individuals alike. Amway, for example, consistently achieves production rates far above national averages, rallies enthusiastic employees in times of difficulty, and has an uncommonly low job-turnover rate.

THAT CHAMPIONSHIP SPIRIT: TOP, Amway's "Nimbleton" tennis tournament pitted U.S. employees against their Australian counterparts, with the U.S. Men's and Australian Women's teams emerging victorious. CENTER, the 1969 Amway Golf League. BOTTOM, one of the many company-sponsored men's softball teams of the 1970s.

Just as Amway managers work to sustain internal harmony with employees, so too do they fully utilize all their resources to build and maintain faith with independent distributors, who come from all walks of life. Numbered among them are attorneys, psychologists, doctors, college students, policemen, housewives, farmers, show business performers, artists, high-school dropouts, writers, ministers, professional athletes, former soldiers, engineers, teachers, and representatives of almost any calling or profession you might name. Despite widely diverse backgrounds, income brackets, and geographical locations, they share one viewpoint in common: a creative, positive approach to life and the conviction that Amway contributes to and enhances that productive and optimistic attitude.

From their earliest business days, Van Andel and DeVos have worked tirelessly to foster that kind of upbeat outlook and performance. When meeting with distributors and encouraging them to greater achievement, they are also constantly maintaining a dialogue so that they can be aware of individual problems and anxieties, whether existing or potential. How is this possible now that the rallies and conventions, which began as small, intimate get-togethers, have become regional, national, and international gatherings of many thousands of people?

The answer lies in the family-oriented structure of the company, one that not only permits, but encourages, individuals to express themselves. Although emotions run high and excitement sometimes creates "an electric arc between the motivational speakers and their cheering audience," there is almost invariably a constructive dialogue that is provocative and valuable.

Van Andel and DeVos are constantly outspoken in counseling distributors to look beyond themselves to what is best for their communities. An effective distributor, they assert, is bound to be a booster. "A city is not a *thing*," insists DeVos. "It's hundreds or thousands or millions of people, each one doing something. Number yourself among those who are being constructive, not just by contributing to charities and cultural groups, but by cleaning up litter, speaking well of your neighborhood, talking with pride about your job — telling everyone you meet that this is a great place to live in and you're going to help make a difference."

Time and again, it has been well-documented that Amway people *have* made a difference — often an enormous one — in the nature and development of their communities. What could be a better way to see this concept come alive than through the profiles of some people who are outstanding in their accomplishments, yet typical of the Amway concept of living and working.

"AN ELECTRIC ARC": Enthusiasm is the hallmark of Amway's distributors' meetings, as is apparent at Crown Direct Distributor Bernice Hansen's weekly motivational and sales training meetings.

FRANK AND RITA DELISLE

Although the year 1959 was an auspicious one for Rich DeVos and Jay Van Andel as they laid the foundation for Amway, it seemed anything but lucky for Frank and Rita Delisle. The first setback came when the Massachusetts printing shop where Frank worked was abruptly closed following the death of the owner. Unable to find suitable work as a printer, Frank decided to pack his wife and four young children into the family car and seek better opportunities in California. Fate, however, had another blow in store. En route, the moving van containing most of the Delisles' possessions caught fire, leaving them to start their "new life" with no furniture, few clothes or accessories, and mounting debts.

Illnesses added to their woes later that year, including several large hospital bills that were not covered by medical insurance. Three years of hardship and struggle brought the family closer together than ever, but resulted in very little improvement in their finances or way of life.

The turning point came, also unexpectedly, during a visit to the home of Rita's sister, who introduced them to a business opportunity called Amway. It was New Year's Day and Frank was too preoccupied with the football games to pay much attention. But his attention was quickly brought into focus when the enthusiastic Rita later told him in detail about the opportunities that existed.

FAMILY ALBUM: TOP RIGHT, Frank and Rita Delisle. BOTTOM RIGHT, Triple Diamond Direct Distributors Dennis and Sharon Delisle. ABOVE, son Frank and daughter-in-law Barb, Double Diamond Direct Distributors.

Today, Amway is a family affair in the attractive small town of Morgan Hill, California, where they live. Not only have Frank and Rita long since become Crown Ambassadors, but they can point proudly to three other Delisle distributorships and a platoon of grandchildren that ensure that Amway will not be without Delisles for generations to come!

Son Frank and daughter-in-law Barbara are Double Diamonds. Son Dennis and his wife, Sharon, are Triple Diamonds, while their son, David, manages the business. Daughter Debbie recently started a distributorship in San Diego and Rita's mother, in her mid-eighties, is a Direct Distributor.

Frank and Rita never tried to persuade their children to join Amway. "My advice is to leave the kids alone," says Rita, "but praise them a lot. We had them work with us when they were young and we exposed them to all the nice people in the business. They saw that Amway paid off and took care of us."

As the children grew up, they pursued their own interests. Frank Jr. studied architectural engineering and Dennis graduated from college with a degree in accounting and secondary education. Both, however, started with Amway in their late teens on a part-time basis and became Direct Distributors while they were still students. Their success led them right back to Amway every time they considered going into their chosen fields of study.

"The best thing Mom and Dad did for us," says Dennis, who recently built a $750,000 Amway office complex, "was to give us our freedom — freedom to fail and freedom to succeed. We know the pain and struggle they went through to build the business. We respect their achievements because we know they did not come about overnight. Amway helped all of us to grow in many ways and has brought our family together and kept it close."

"In most family businesses there's competition and rivalry," comments Frank Sr. "But that's not true with Amway, since we each have our own business. We can talk about rallies and the next meeting, but we don't have to outdo each other. Amway brings us together. It's the common denominator in our lives."

LIVING THE DREAM: TOP, Frank and Rita Delisle on the balcony of their Morgan Hill, California, home. CENTER, Dennis and Sharon Delisle and their family carry on the family tradition — and the Amway dream — in California. BOTTOM, Dennis Delisle's latest project, a $750,000 Amway office complex.

DEXTER AND BIRDIE YAGER

In 1964, when he first heard about Amway, Dexter Yager was making $95 a week and his wife, Birdie, had her hands full trying to manage four young children. Then a friend of Birdie's asked if Dex would mind listening to an explanation of the Amway Sales and Marketing Plan. Desperate and clutching at straws, Dex decided to abandon his unrewarding job as a salesman for a local brewery and take a stab at this new venture.

Prospects looked great when the Yagers soon qualified as Direct Distributors. But then business leveled off and for the next three years the Yagers always seemed to be pedaling harder than ever but getting nowhere. "We were doing the work," recalls Dex, "but nothing was happening." They still lived in an old row house in Rome, New York, and had to depend upon a ten-year-old "rotted out" station wagon for family transportation.

It was at this crucial juncture that Dex happened to read a book on positive thinking. He realized that he had been looking at Amway as just another salesman's job and had never grasped the real philosophies and objectives that make Amway unique. "I saw that what we needed was to develop a new dream," he says. "About that same time," he adds, "we were also getting tired of shoveling all that snow in northern New York. So we decided to move south."

After doing some geographical homework, the Yagers selected the area around Charlotte, North Carolina. They settled there in 1969, with a family that now included six children. Dex put his newfound philosophy to work — and things quickly began to turn around.

Today, the Yagers live in a sprawling, colonial-style home in Pineville, North Carolina, where the small-town environment blends Southern charm with gracious living. Despite their relaxed life-style, Dex is a hardworking individual who is constantly striving to expand the business, attract new achievers, and add dimensions to his way of life. "Most of the hours in my day are devoted to business," he says, "and even our social and family life revolve around some phase of Amway or the other business ventures in which we have invested."

FORMULA FOR SUCCESS: OPPOSITE, TOP, *Dexter and Birdie Yager enjoy the holidays in their Pineville, North Carolina, home.* OPPOSITE, CENTER, *getting the message at a 1985 meeting of the Diamond Club.* OPPOSITE, BOTTOM, *an outward sign of achievement.* LEFT, *the inner glow of success.*

All seven of the Yagers' sons and daughters are actively involved in the business, too. When the children were young, they helped take orders and stock the shelves. Now that they are older — ranging in age from 18 to 27 — they too have become Amway distributors. "It's marvelous," says Birdie, "the way this business allows children to work at home with their parents, to learn the work ethic from someone who loves them."

One of the most significant messages that Dex has for his children, and for the people he recruits into Amway, is that they can be both dreamer and realist at the same time. "Success is the practical result of a worthwhile dream," he explains. "People often wander through life with emotional goals, not logical ones. What they must do is to set a goal and then go and claim it, as though it were already theirs. When they work toward their dream as though there were no way they could *not* get it, then they surely will."

It is readily apparent that Dex and Birdie have realized a good many of their dreams. They qualified as Crown Direct Distributors in 1981. They have achieved enough financial success to diversify and invest substantially in restaurants, a hotel, a bank, and other real estate holdings. They have both the means and the freedom to travel anywhere in the world at any time. They can schedule their own hours and live where they want. They can afford tennis courts, pools, boats, and an antique automobile collection.

Yet, with all of this affluence, one of their greatest joys is the opportunity to pass along the "success formula" to others. To this end, Dex has not only lectured to audiences far and wide but has authored a number of books on attitudes, business philosophies, and ways of enriching one's life. His inspirational messages are put to good use not only by Amway distributors but by people of all ages and all walks of life who are trying to clarify and reach their goals.

And people, after all, remain the most important element of the Yagers' dream. "The things we are most grateful for," says Dex, "are the personal growth and the friendships that come with it. If money was all there was to it, we would have retired several years ago. To us, the relationships we have developed lie far above the dollars. The greatest rewards are not getting something yourself, but seeing others get it."

STAN AND RUTH EVANS

When they were featured in an article in *Amagram* magazine in 1973, Stan and Ruth Evans had just become Triple Diamond Direct Distributors after eight years with Amway. "Our success only represents what's available for every Amway distributor who wants it enough to work for it," they said at the time. *"Nothing* pays off like work!"

Stan and Ruth were accustomed to work. They raised beef cattle for many years in Nebraska, an occupation that kept them on the go from sunup to sundown. Yet, from the standpoint of future achievement, they seemed unlikely candidates for success when they first joined Amway. For one thing, they lived in a remote, thinly populated area. They were four miles from their closest neighbor and 14 miles from the nearest town — which had a population of only 240. It was hardly the location for a business that is so dependent upon close association and communication with other people. They could not even expect much help from their sponsor, Stan's cousin, who lived 200 miles away!

Another drawback was the fact that Stan and Ruth were not at all outgoing or at ease with strangers. "We were both so shy," Ruth recalls, "that it was painful for us to be in even a small group of people."

When they attended their first Amway convention, they were so self-conscious that they could not bring themselves to walk up on the stage to receive their Ruby Direct Distributor pins from Jay Van Andel and Rich DeVos. But their outlook and attitudes changed very quickly as they became more and more confident and began to realize that Amway was like a large, supportive family. In one sense, their initial shyness was a blessing in disguise. It gave them insight to encourage and inspire new distributors who also are not too sure of themselves. "Our most important goal in life is to help these people, just as we were helped," says Stan, "and to see them develop and experience personal growth the way we did."

As their business expanded, Stan and Ruth could see the even greater potential that lay before them. In the summer of 1967, they moved to Wray, Colorado, a community of some 2,000 people that would become their permanent hometown. It was evident by now

NEW HORIZONS: *ABOVE, Crown Direct Distributors Stan and Ruth Evans.* OPPOSITE, *the Evans family's Cadillac, one of the first cars presented in Amway's automobile awards program.*

that their career and future lay with Amway. In less than a year and a half, their Amway income was equaling that of the best of their ranch years.

One of the factors that helped inspire their success was the realization that Amway offered many of the finest products on the market — products they could promote and market proudly and with confidence. With that growing self-assurance, they made it a point to attend company seminars and conventions and to participate to the fullest extent. They earned their way into Amway's prestigious Diamond Club, and Stan served on the Board of Directors of the Amway Distributors Association. They became Crown Direct Distributors in March 1979, at which time — in sharp contrast to their first year with Amway — they were described as "poised" and "confident," in a manner that "befits their exalted position among Amway's top distributors."

Meanwhile, they found the time to raise a family of three boys and a girl, and today all their children participate in the business. Pam, age 23, who is married, is the most active distributor. Brent, 26, and Gary, 24, are also distributors, while Jay, 14, acts as stock clerk.

The Evans family lives in a luxurious home in Wray that presents quite a contrast to their modest, somewhat rustic ranch home in Haigler. The decision to go with Amway has not only enhanced the life-style of the entire family, but has made it possible for them to spend summers together at a lake, make use of their private plane, and take trips all over the world. "We fly from one end of the world to the other," says Stan, "whereas in the past our vacations were limited to once-a-year trips to visit relatives in the mountains some 200 miles away."

For Stan and Ruth, one of the most important results of their success with Amway has been the opportunity to help others. Of course, they do this constantly by bringing newcomers into the Amway business and by encouraging those who are already distributors to achieve even greater results. But they also contribute a great deal of time and financial support to causes that they feel are worthy. For example, they provide financial support for four foster children overseas. And they have provided generous assistance to the Teen Challenge Center in Birmingham, Alabama, a remarkably successful drug rehabilitation facility operated under the direction of Ruth's brother.

Stan and Ruth feel that Amway has had some great new developments lately. "Because of the excitement generated by new products and new horizons," says Stan, "we're more involved than we ever were. The future has always looked good, from one year to the next. But now it has reached a new crest. The old Amway is still there, the spirit and the challenge and the people. But new excitement has been added and the future looks better than it ever has before."

BILL AND PEGGY BRITT

Would an overworked city manager studying for a master's degree in public administration and serving as an active officer in the National Guard be a good candidate for a career with Amway? While the answer in some people's minds would probably be no, in the case of Bill Britt it is a most emphatic yes. His story is one more example that illustrates that successful Amway distributors can come from just about any place under the sun.

It was in 1970 that Bill made the decision that was to change his life. After returning from military service, he held the position of assistant city manager for Raleigh, the state capital of North Carolina. He was also a graduate student at North Carolina State University, taking courses in politics and government. His wife, Peggy, worked as a secretary for the Carolina Power and Light Company.

Bill describes himself — then and now — as "a real workaholic," who preferred working to socializing but who still did not achieve the status or income he wanted. He was described by others as "a take-charge type, a hard-nosed, no-nonsense leader with emphatic opinions and no reluctance to express them." Yet behind this tough facade was a person who was caring and sympathetic and who genuinely liked people. Perhaps that's why he felt there was something missing in his administrative career and why he jumped at the opportunity when he was introduced to Amway.

"I immediately became excited," he recalls. "I had spent three years looking for an opportunity that would solve our economic problems, and I had just about given up. I'd checked into many different opportunities, but nothing excited me like Amway. I was proud to be part of it from the very beginning because I believed it to be honest and ethical, and it was so flexible that I could fit the work in with the other things I was doing."

Bill continued working in city government when he started with Amway. For two years he held the position of city manager of Goldsboro, North Carolina. He also managed to find the time to earn his master's degree. When asked how he juggled a full-time job, attended college, spent time as a military officer, and built an Amway business, Bill acknowledges that he always did have an inexhaustible capacity for burning the midnight oil.

Peggy has always helped Bill by taking on secretarial jobs with the hope that he would have a little more time for the education he felt was vital to success. Yet when the Amway opportunity arrived, her enthusiasm was less than his and her participation more gradual. "I learned the business by helping Bill," she recalls. "But the excitement grew more slowly. What really made me appreciate Amway was the growing realization that this new life-style made it possible for us to spend much more time together. Before Amway came into the picture, Bill was always so busy that I just never seemed to hold as much of a place in his life as I really wanted."

WONDERFUL CHANGES: ABOVE, Triple Diamond Direct Distributors Bill and Peggy Britt. OPPOSITE, LEFT, for Bill, Amway has meant gracious living and personal growth. OPPOSITE, RIGHT, the Britts' magnificent Chapel Hill home.

Peggy started out by taking care of ordering, stocking, and distributing the products. She was greatly encouraged by the fact that Amway provided top quality products that were easy to promote and sell. "We had to put up with the cartons and products all over the house," she says, "and the traffic of people coming and going, of course. But that has all changed now because we have outside offices and storage space, and we have full-time help."

After becoming Direct Distributors in 1970, Bill and Peggy Britt rapidly earned additional qualifications, becoming Triple Diamond Direct Distributors in 1980. Along the way they have build an impressive, world-wide organization and are known for their continual investment of time and energy in well-attended rallies

and conventions. Having their own plane and full-time pilot makes travel easy and comfortable. When not on the road or in the air, they enjoy a magnificent home in the gracious old college town of Chapel Hill, nestled in a woodland setting at the foot of the Piedmont Plateau.

Bill is still a workaholic and always will be. "Amway is not only my career, but my hobby, my avocation, and my social life," he says. His former interest in government has been transferred, too, to Amway, and he serves as a member of the Board of Directors of the Amway Distributors Association and is a participant in the company's ongoing activities on behalf of free enterprise and other national issues.

"We don't need anything else," he explains, "because we enjoy the whole Amway family and we visit with Amway people all over, wherever they are assembling and wherever the action is."

Above all, though, the Britts are people-oriented. That's why they have been so successful in taking the dream of Amway and making it a reality for so many others. "Amway means a great deal to me," says Bill. "It changed me. Before Amway, I used to love things and use people. Now I've learned how to love people and use things. I've seen wonderful changes happening to lots of people since I first came into this business."

POSITIVE ATTITUDES: Triple Diamond Direct Distributors George and Ruth Halsey in Ada on Halsey Day, March 18, 1980.

GEORGE AND RUTH HALSEY

A quarter of a century ago, when Amway was a fledgling business, George Halsey was a stock clerk in a Bronx shoe store and his wife, Ruth, was at home with their two children, Karen and John. Although hardworking and upwardly mobile, neither of them had any illusions about finding a way to sudden wealth. It was not surprising, then, that when they were introduced to Amway in the spring of 1975, they — especially Ruth — were skeptical.

"I had never heard of Amway," she laughs, "and I'd never seen so much as a single product. I just didn't believe that the Plan had much promise and I certainly wasn't going to give anyone $36 for a kit!"

Contrary to this initial judgment, Ruth decided to commit herself to the business after talking with distributors she met at a rally and becoming inspired while hearing Rich DeVos's "Selling America" tape recording. George responded quickly to her growing enthusiasm, and by fall the Halseys had qualified as Direct Distributors. Within two years, Ruth was convinced that Amway was really for them and made the decision to resign from her post as a physical education teacher so they could pursue their goal: a Diamond Direct Distributorship.

"For a long time," explains George, "blacks did not feel that they could make it in any business. We wanted to prove them wrong. We wanted to put some blacks in *Amagram* magazine and be recognized."

And they did. Although the Halseys manage what they refer to as a "very integrated" organization, they make special efforts throughout the year to familiarize other blacks with the Amway opportunity. "Minorities join Amway for the same reasons anyone else does," says George, while his wife adds, "We always made a big effort to develop trust with our distributors and we always told them we would help every step of the way." The Halseys, who now live in North Carolina, have been very successful in their efforts — they are Triple Diamond Direct Distributors.

The rewards, both personal and financial, have been great. While they are grateful for their enhanced life-style and the opportunities they never had before to enjoy the finer things of life, they feel that what makes them really glow is to see how other peoples' lives change for the better because of Amway.

"I've seen people get promotions because their attitude on the job improves after Amway," says George. "This business brings families closer and I've noticed great changes in the children — they believe in themselves because they are surrounded by positive attitudes at home."

SHARING THE OPPORTUNITY: LEFT, *the Halseys at a 1985 meeting of the Diamond Club.* BELOW, *George and Ruth relax with family and friends.*

JIM AND SHARON JANZ

A few people are lucky enough to choose the right career — one that's rewarding and lets them live and work where they want. Jim and Sharon Janz are among those few. They have been able to share the best of both worlds ever since they became an Amway family more than two decades ago. They live in the small town of Surrey near Vancouver in British Columbia. They're close enough to the city to enjoy its amenities, but far enough away to work and play in an environment that is both stimulating and gracious.

The story begins in 1964 when Jim decided that his job as a teacher, while satisfying in its own way, gave him little opportunity for raising a family the way he wanted to. After listening to the advice of a friend who kept suggesting that he look into Amway, he finally agreed to give it a try. "I had to do something," he recalls. "We were literally borrowing to stay alive. We lived in a tiny basement apartment and tried to make do with secondhand furniture and a car that was always breaking down." To complicate matters, they already had one infant to feed and clothe and Sharon was expecting a second. It was not exactly what Jim had dreamed of as the ideal situation for his family.

Joining Amway did not solve all of their financial problems overnight. Very few people in the region had heard of Amway or its products, and Jim quickly found that he had to set his goals carefully and plan ahead. But he could tell that Amway offered remarkable opportunities for people who wanted to get more out of life than simply a job and a place to hang their hat.

"I could see in Amway," says Jim, "a way for us to attain true financial security in just a few years. We decided that we really wanted to succeed." With the help of Sharon, who at first had to spend most of her time raising their first two children, they attained Diamond status by the spring of 1965. The Double Diamond pin was not so easy. "We tried 12 times before we made it," says Jim, "but the important fact is that we kept on trying and were determined to reach our goal."

MAKING IT HAPPEN: TOP, Crown Ambassador Direct Distributors Jim and Sharon Janz. RIGHT, helping others reach their goals, at a Janz distributor rally. OPPOSITE, the Janzes attend an assembly of Amway Hong Kong distributors.

In the same spirit of determination, Jim and Sharon eventually became Crown Ambassador Direct Distributors — the first in Canada — some 14 years after joining Amway. As a matter of fact, they became the first distributors in Amway history to achieve both Triple Diamond and Crown Direct Distributor awards in the *same month*.

From a material standpoint, their life in Amway has been totally rewarding. The basement apartment has now become an elegant and stately mansion that they describe as looking like something out of *Gone with the Wind*. The Janzes also enjoy a magnificent vacation condominium in Washington.

Over and beyond these amenities, however, Jim and Sharon feel that the greatest asset has been the opportunity to develop a healthy, vigorous, and meaningful family life. "Thanks to our Amway business," says Sharon, "we are able to work and play together as a family. That's the beauty of Amway. It's flexible and you are free to plan your living around your family, rather than having the family constantly trying to accommodate itself to a rigid nine-to-five routine.

"We can take time off when our children have school vacations or holidays. We can go skiing, or boating, or simply get together for family recreation at home."

One of the enviable rewards of having an Amway life-style has been the opportunity for all six Janzes to travel together and see the world. They have been to Europe, Asia, the Caribbean, and other exotic places, as well as much of the United States and Canada.

"This is one of my greatest pleasures," says Jim, "to be able to see the world together and profit from our experiences as a family. We could never have done this if I had been in the conventional type of job — and certainly not on a teacher's salary, even with extended summer vacations."

With such a full life, it would seem that Sharon and Jim would have little time for other activities. Yet both are active in community affairs and in their church. Jim is president of Living Bible of Canada and chairman of the Robert Schuller Ministry of Canada. He is also currently chairman of the Amway Distributors Association of Canada.

For those who envy the Janzes' achievements and feel that success is a matter of luck and being in the right place at the right time, Jim has this to say: "Success is primarily a matter of having clearly defined goals and a consistent, day-by-day plan for reaching those goals. If you aim at nothing, I guarantee that you'll hit nothing. But if you believe, as I do, that whatever your mind can conceive you can achieve, then you are really going to make it happen."

These are the kinds of people and concepts that have made Amway strong and self-sustaining.

The stage is set for the filming of a 1983 Amway television commercial.

Chapter Six

INCENTIVES AND INNOVATIONS

"The incentive of business is to make a profit. The objective of business is not to make a profit but to serve a need."
— *James F. Lincoln*

The story is told about a young salesman for a radio network who made the rounds in towns served by one of the stations with the idea of signing up some of the small businesses for commercials. Driving by the local general store in one small village, he decided from the poor condition of the building that here was one merchant who really needed to talk up his wares in order to improve his business.

"No thanks, son," he was told curtly by the owner. "Been in business 35 years and everyone in town already knows what kinds of products I'm selling."

"I see," replied the salesman, turning and gazing down the street. "By the way, what is that big building down there at the edge of town?"

"Oh, that's our church," beamed the grocer proudly. "Got the biggest congregation anywhere in the county!"

"Hmmm," mused the salesman out loud, "then I wonder why they bother to keep on ringing the bell."

The message, of course, is that *you* may know very well what kinds of products you have to sell, and some of your prospective customers may have an idea of what they are, but if you don't "ring the bell" and remind people of their needs, a lot of the products and services you have to offer are *never* going to get sold.

It is a well-documented fact that L.O.C. Cleaner, which was Amway's first, and for a time its only, product in 1959 was successful for three basic reasons. First, it was an *excellent product*, an unusually effective all-purpose cleaning liquid; second, its consumers had *a real need* for this kind of product; and third, the new company's distributors went out and told prospective buyers how good it really was.

Over the years, the same success story was repeated as Van Andel and DeVos carefully investigated and selected new products to add to the line. These early products not only became popular quickly, but proved to be enduring. In 1979, for example, 19 years after it had first been introduced, S-A-8 Laundry Detergent was ranked *first* in consumer brand loyalty from among more than 40 competitive brands. Dish Drops® Dishwashing Liquid achieved the same recognition when compared with more than 19 leading competitors.

It was apparent to Van Andel and DeVos from the beginning that their distributors would need constant additions of new products, as well as increasing supplies of the already established lines. Van Andel assumed early responsibility for product development, working at first on his own but gradually building a knowledgeable staff around him. A Product Development Committee was formed, which he chaired, and later a more diversified Product Review Committee.

Those embryonic years were not without their growing pains, DeVos recalls. "We didn't know whether the numbers were right or wrong, whether the idea itself could work, or whether the products would be acceptable to consumers. What direction should we take? High-ticket items? Low-ticket items? At first it was trial and error. We experimented with everything from automobile generators and water conditioners to fallout shelters. And in the meantime, we kept selling soap."

The story of the 110-volt automobile generators was a typical example of trial and error. They were supplied by a man in Colorado who built them himself and thus could offer them at a good, competitive price. He would produce enough to fill an immediate order, load up his roomy Cadillac with them, and drive the shipment to Ada, then head back home and repeat the cycle.

"It was a good product," recalls Kay Evans, "but we had a hard time getting enough to sell. I'd arrive at the office first thing in the morning and there he'd be sitting, with his Cadillac loaded up like nobody's business. The back bumper would be about two inches off the ground."

But the disadvantages soon outnumbered the assets of the product. Besides the problems of haphazard supply, the generator had to be promoted with care, since it did not function properly in all makes and models of automobiles. A year or so after it was introduced, with a dwindling number of distributors interested in handling the product, it was dropped from the line.

The water conditioning unit was another case in point, though for different reasons. At the outset, it appeared to be a superior product, an automatic machine and an innovation by comparison with other brands of that time that were rental units or at best required periodic manual servicing. As Amway's product literature convinced prospective customers, "You don't rent a refrigerator, stove, or water heater.

CLASSIC LINES: BELOW, *early products.* OPPOSITE, *the complete line of Amway Home Care and Personal Care products, from a decade ago.*

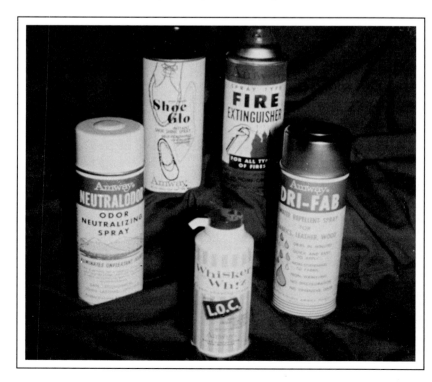

Why rent a water softener?" Satisfaction was assured because samples of local water from each purchaser or prospect were sent to the company's research department for analysis and precise recommendations for proper conditioning. Despite these assets, the installation and servicing created too many chronic headaches for distributors. After coping with the problems and finding no real solutions, the company reluctantly scratched the product from its list.

The underground fallout shelter was a different story, but with the same ending. In the early 1960s, with escalating public concern over the possibility of global warfare, the shelter found ready acceptance. "Built like a battleship," as the sales literature guaranteed, the shelter was "designed to give maximum protection from fallout in the event of nuclear war." However, as East-West tensions subsided, so did consumer interest and the product became outdated.

At the other extreme were the products that literally were *too* popular. Distributors sold certain items with such enthusiasm and drive that the demand was constantly exceeding the supply. As the clamor for them increased, the company raced ahead on a program to construct more facilities. "Continuous, hurried expansion led to buildings and structures that looked like a series of lean-tos," DeVos recalls. "Each unit sort of hung on to the next one." Van Andel likens the situation to that of "the dog being wagged by the tail."

Riding the coattails of popularity, Amway became known as "the soap company" because its selection and timing of cleaning products were precisely on target. The late 1950s and early 1960s proved to be milestone years in the "wash-and-wear" revolution fomented by the American clothing industry. Stepping right into the burgeoning demand, Amway's detergents realistically promised two distinct advantages. The

SHOWCASE OF STARS: OPPOSITE, *a continuing evolution, as product packaging and quality keep getting better and better.* ABOVE, *one scene from the product display in Amway's second-generation Showcase bus, which took to the roads in 1965 to bring Amway products to people all across America.*

first was their ability to clean polyester and resin-treated fabrics. The second was their capacity, because they were biodegradable, for doing the job *without* polluting the environment.

TURNING PRODUCTS INTO PROFITS

Right along, one of the keys to successful sales has been the fact that distributors themselves are among the most enthusiastic users of Amway products. Some distributors have even gone so far as to invent new and different ways for using certain products. In fact, a regular feature for many years in the company publication, *Amagram*, told about these remarkable "distributor discoveries."

One distributor, for example, informed readers that Shoe Glo Shoe Shine Spray not only protected shoes but could be sprayed on carbon copies to prevent them

from smearing, would protect cork products from chipping, and could preserve live floral arrangements beyond their normal life expectancy. Also publicized was the story of the tire dealer who had purchased the product, not for its intended purpose, but to add luster to the tires he kept on display.

Other distributors have discovered that Amway® Silver Polish cleans grout, that Amway® Car Wash enhances painted woodwork and venetian blinds, and that Buff-Up® Furniture Polish is a natural for keeping the decks of fiberglass boats looking like new. A veterinarian swore (though Amway recommended against it) that an application of Wonder Mist® Silicone Lubricant worked wonders when it came to grooming the tangled coats of dogs. Of all the Amway products for which new and imaginative uses have been invented, probably none can compare, however, with L.O.C. Cleaner. Two cupfuls in a pail of water

INDUSTRY LEADER: TOP, Orville Hoxie joins Van Andel and DeVos in cutting the ribbon to officially open Amway's new cosmetics plant. BOTTOM and OPPOSITE, surgical cleanliness and precision meet state-of-the-art technology in the Ada-based facility.

will remove wallpaper. One teaspoon dissolved in a quart of water and applied to houseplants once a month will keep the leaves greener. The detergent will also remove the smell of onions from hands and deodorize utensils and implements that have been in contact with fresh-caught fish.

Needless to say, Amway published these imaginative tidbits of information from distributors only when adding a cautionary disclaimer that the company assumed no responsibility for the effectiveness or results of such applications.

One area, though, where imagination and innovation have paid off in a practical and profitable way has been in the marketing of Amway's distinctive line of Artistry Cosmetics. "Any Man Can Sell Beauty Products" assured an editorial that effectively deflated the old myth that this aspect of selling was solely "a woman's world." Supporting this thesis was Bill Shaw, whose distributorship has enjoyed notable success in moving the Artistry line.

"Men can sell cosmetics as well as women can," he says, "and in many cases even better than women. In fact, any man can sell makeup. A woman respects a man's opinion. When he says that he likes a certain shade of lipstick or that his wife just loves a particular item, he's already made the sale!"

If the prospective customer says she prefers to stick with the brand she has been using, Shaw has a ready and convincing response. He pauses for a moment and then says, "I was standing here thinking how much *more* beautiful you'd be if you used Artistry."

In order to meet the expanding demands for the Artistry line, Amway in 1983 opened a new Ada-based cosmetics plant equipped with the latest state-of-the-art manufacturing equipment. It has an environmentally controlled atmosphere that controls dust and bacteria. In addition, Artistry experts each year conduct hundreds of cosmetic and skin-care workshops in the United States and abroad.

Since the very beginnings of Amway, successful distributors have displayed ingenuity and imagination in selling all product lines. They have done so, in part, because they have had one asset in common: the ability to think in terms of the products they see before them and then project themselves into the minds of prospective customers.

Vince Gaffey of Illinois typifies this approach. He was one of the early distributors, starting with Nutrilite in 1950. When Amway introduced L.O.C. Cleaner in 1959, he and a partner each took home two cases to their wives. "We figured if we couldn't sell it, we could at least use it ourselves," he explains. When they discovered how superior the product was, Vince and his wife, Alice, who had joined him in Amway, were easily able to convince their prospects that it was one of the best buys in town.

NEW PRODUCTS, NEW GOALS

Besides the highly successful detergents, Amway's early product lines included a glass cleaner, germicidal concentrate, polymer floor wax, wax remover, and several automobile-care items, including a low-acid replacement electrolyte for storage batteries. Then there was a unique hair-color product named Formula 1886 that could be combed into the hair to restore the color over a period of one to two weeks, rather than with a startling overnight change. A line of stainless steel cookware also received strong billing on the part of some distributors, since it could be handled exclusively and sold on either a full- or part-time basis. Queen™ Cookware is still a mainstay of the Amway line.

All of these items, and every product bearing the Amway name, carried a 100 percent money-back guarantee.

"Jay and Rich were adamant that *everything* be 100 percent," explains Kay Evans, recalling the decision by Van Andel and DeVos to undertake their own manufacturing and commit themselves to top quality in every way. "Whether it was the way you made the product or sold it or presented it or stood behind it, everything had to be right."

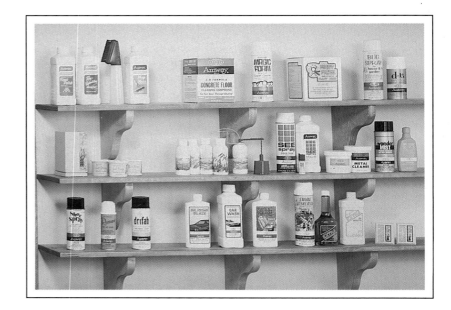

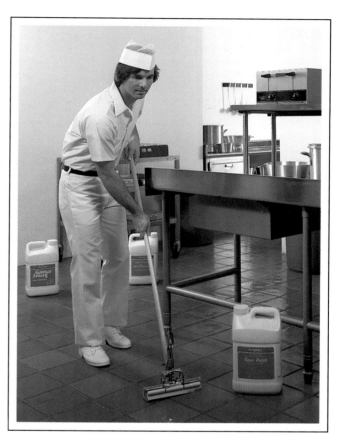

TOTAL SATISFACTION: An array of Amway products — some "classics" and some new to the line — all guaranteeing customers 100 percent satisfaction or their money back.

MEETING A WORLD OF NEEDS: Amway's extensive line includes products in seven different groups, or "businesses": Home Care, Personal Care, Health & Fitness, HomeTech, Catalog, Commercial, and Services.

Even the earliest testing methods bore testimony to their intense personal commitment. The two founders would first use new products themselves, often putting them to tests they might never be subjected to by average users. If they decided they liked a product, they would then produce a sample run and make it available to distributors. Now it was out of their hands to make personal judgments. If distributor or customer response was negative, the product was either discontinued or improved to the point of total acceptability.

This rudimentary and unsophisticated approach to research and development was surprisingly effective, judging by the way some of the early products have endured and continued to be heavily in demand. Yet, of necessity, as the company grew and management had to evaluate not just a few dozen but hundreds of products each year, more scientific methods were devised. Today's new products must do more than pass muster with the company's top executives. Thousands of dollars and sometimes many years of study are committed to researching a product before it is approved for marketing.

The research and development procedures not only apply to the investigation and testing of new products, but to the continuing improvement of existing lines and the streamlining of manufacturing operations to keep production up and costs down. S-A-8 Laundry Detergent, for example, has undergone numerous improvements and, says Tom Edwards, director and R&D associate - special projects, "We are still making changes. As technology advances, the product gets better and better."

How extensive is R&D? Figures do not tell the whole story, but they help. During 1982, for instance, the research staff in Ada analyzed 425,000 bits of information while completing evaluation tests on some 32,000 new product samples. In 1983, the company's Quality Assurance Inspectors logged more than 122,000 hours just in checking to make certain that Amway products were right *before* they were cleared for market.

PASSING MUSTER: TOP, research scientist at work in Amway's Analytical Services Laboratory. CENTER, one of many multifaceted laboratories in the R&D center in Ada. BOTTOM, R&D Nutrition lab personnel sample the fruits of their labor. OPPOSITE, Amway scientists and research personnel hard at work creating, analyzing, testing, questioning, finding answers.

COMMITMENT TO QUALITY: TOP LEFT, *Eric Van Dellen at work in the Analytical Lab.* BOTTOM LEFT, *Mimi Brophy perfects Nutrilite Food Bars in Amway's Nutrition Lab.* ABOVE, *birthplace of quality, Amway's Research & Development Building.* OPPOSITE, *introduced in 1960 and still a product line leader, S-A-8 Plus Premium Laundry Concentrate keeps getting "better and better."*

If research was unsophisticated during Amway's infancy, manufacturing could be called almost primitive. When production facilities were first installed at Ada, L.O.C. Cleaner was mixed by hand in 40-gallon vats and stirred with a wooden oar. As product demands soared, such methods naturally became unrealistic. Automatic systems were introduced to replace each of the old manufacturing operations.

One of the first new pieces of manufacturing equipment installed was a standard, semiautomatic milk-filling assembly that had been modified to handle liquid detergent. A major step forward occurred in 1961, shortly after Van Andel and DeVos contracted with outside suppliers for four new aerosol products: Neutralodor™ Air Freshener, drifab® Water-Resistant Fabric Spray, Shoe Glo Shoe Shine Spray, and a highly effective fire extinguisher. The sales success of these items prompted Amway to design and install its own aerosol manufacturing plant.

The move was not without problems and hazards. The first aerosol product to come off this new assembly line was Whisker Whiz® Shaving Cream. "It was produced on the filling line by a somewhat laborious process," recalls Bob Rooker, director of shift operations, "whereby one person filled the can and passed it to the next person to have the valve crimped on. The third person down the line injected the gas, while still another worker placed the cans in a basket and dunked them in water to check for leaks." The process produced no more than about 12 cans per minute.

The filling and charging of aerosol containers in those early days had its moments of suspense, if not high drama. "Sometimes the cans would blow up," recalls Wally Buttrick, who for a time was assigned to production. "The workers would overpressurize them and the whole can would just take off like a rocket and go right to the ceiling."

In 1963, George Brock joined Amway as quality control technical director, the same title he had held with his previous employer, a Chicago aerosol firm. "The potential you people have here at Amway is phenomenal," he said at the time. "Yesterday you had a concept for a new product; today you create it; tomorrow you package it; and in a week it's in the hands of customers!"

Although he readily acknowledged that he was compressing the truth a bit, there was no doubt that a lot of action was taking place in this area of operations. On the assembly line, for example, the rate of production had been accelerated to 170 cans per minute.

The growing success of aerosol manufacturing and sales that year made it advisable to design and construct a tank farm for the storage of propellants. This step in turn prompted Amway, during the next two years, to expand the line of aerosol products to 26, including such items as a hand cleaner, weed killer, insect spray, laundry starch, window cleaner, silicone lubricant, and personal care items like deodorant, cologne, and hair spray.

A JOY FOREVER: *Artistry Cosmetics and Jewelry — beauty products designed "for the fashion-conscious woman of today."*

The midsixties saw the introduction of dozens of new products, all of which had been carefully researched, designed, and market-tested. Among them were newly formulated hand and body lotions, baby oil and powder, improved shampoos, iron-on patches, and a fabric softener. A major shift in product lines was destined by 1968. Mail-order selling had firmly established itself as a gigantic business and personal care products and cosmetics had become billion-dollar industries. Studying these significant trends, Amway focused directly on market needs by introducing the Artistry Cosmetics line and by creating the Personal Shoppers Catalog.

The market was strong enough for Amway to allocate three million dollars (in 1968 dollars) to the Artistry Cosmetics line alone, a sum that represented its largest single investment up to that time in any single product line. Artistry Cosmetics were packaged in distinctive, designer-created containers, offering women everything they desired, from eye makeup and nail polish to face powder, beauty oil, skin creams, and more than 35 shades of lipstick. Two new fragrance lines were soon added: Per Chance for women, with perfume, colognes, bath oil, body splashes, soaps, and powders; and Silver Surf® Toiletries for men, with items that included after-shave lotion, colognes, talcum, and hair-grooming aids.

These products, supplemented by a new order system that made it easier to request items singly instead of by the case, motivated distributors to snap up Artistry Cosmetics so quickly that the various products were in short supply for months on end.

The Personal Shoppers Catalog introduced at this time became an immediate "best-seller." Printed in full color and 44 pages in length, it illustrated 300 different products. One delighted recipient called the publication "my dream book in living color." Another complained that "I never can lay hands on my copy. Someone's always borrowing it."

One of the welcome advantages of the catalog was that the items displayed in it could be sold by distributors in the same way as in the past, yet they need not stock the merchandise themselves. Orders were shipped directly to the purchaser from Ada. The plan was great for distributors, but almost caused a crisis at first for the new Catalog Department. Because of the chronic space shortages as business outpaced construction, the department was temporarily housed in truck trailers and in one of those "instant" buildings roofed over by plastic that had to be kept inflated by an air pump.

Fortunately, within a year the department had moved into a huge new distribution center in Ada. Today it enjoys the reputation of being one of the largest catalog businesses in North America.

MAKING DREAMS COME TRUE: A busy distribution center in Ada handles orders for items from the Personal Shoppers Catalog, Amway's "dream book in living color."

SHIFTING INTO HIGH GEAR

The fire which destroyed one of the company's plants in 1969 reinforced a policy of planning and building for safety whenever structures or equipment were replaced. The new mixing plant, laid out to accommodate manufacturing facilities for liquids, pastes, and powders, was explosion-proof and constructed largely of stainless steel. Much of the machinery had been custom-designed to fill specialized manufacturing demands. The unique paste-mixing apparatus, for example, assured perfect uniformity when blending one-hundred-pound batches of fine creams and lotions.

As in the case of the buildings and equipment, product packaging has always required constant modernization. During its first decade, the company just could not afford to stock containers in enormous quantities or to contract for custom-made bottles, boxes, and jars. Standard containers and shipping cartons were purchased at the most reasonable and competitive prices. The only elements of distinction were the labels, designed by Jay Van Andel. By the beginning of the 1970s, however, Amway was well on the way to designing and manufacturing (or commissioning) its own packaging. Operations for the in-house production of boxes and cartons began at the end of the 1960s. The company soon was able to manufacture almost any kind of container, from large shipping cartons to miniature cases for cosmetics and a new line of Artisan® Jewelry.

Within two years, these capabilities were enhanced by the addition of blow-molding facilities for the crafting of fine plastic bottles safely and efficiently. One of the results was the design of Amway's unique square bottle, which is not only distinctive and immediately recognizable, but highly cost-effective because it saves space in shipping and warehousing, as well as on customers' shelves. Today, the familiar square bottle is used for eight different products, each appropriately labeled.

STATE OF THE ART: RIGHT, TOP AND BOTTOM, Amway's printing and binding operations in Ada boast some of the most modern facilities in the country. OPPOSITE, TOP LEFT, Amway's computer facility, constantly expanding and modernizing. OPPOSITE, TOP RIGHT, new equipment controls the formulation of S-A-8. OPPOSITE, BOTTOM LEFT, a high-speed bottle and can printer. OPPOSITE, BOTTOM RIGHT, Amway's packaging engineering laboratory.

Although manufacturing and design were now keeping pace with the times, there were still serious problems with modernizing the inventory system.

"All the inventories were kept manually," explains Pat Conlon, a former vice president, "so the only way we knew how much inventory the corporation had was to shut down the entire system the first working day of each month and take inventory by hand. We brought the information into Ada, added the whole thing up, and somewhere around the fifteenth of the month we knew how much inventory we had back on the first day."

When distributors were surveyed to find out what they expected from the supply system, the consensus was that they had to be able to count on product deliveries once a week on a regular basis. To meet their needs, Amway's first step was to retain a distribution consulting firm to investigate bottlenecks and delays and come up with proposals. The study recommended conversion of the central warehousing procedure to a company-operated network of regional warehouses. Following this professional advice in 1972, Amway established Regional Distribution Centers, known as RDCs.

The RDCs were uniform in design and function, thus standardizing the entire warehousing operation. Today, all-metal shelving for storage is built to accommodate standard 40-by-48 pallets, which also fit exactly inside the semitrailer trucks. Merchandise is placed on pallets in Ada, loaded into the "semis," delivered to the appropriate RDC, and then transferred directly to the shelves.

Products for Amway's foreign operations are also shipped, most frequently by freighters, to the various countries, whose warehousing designs and facilities are comparable to those in the United States. "The

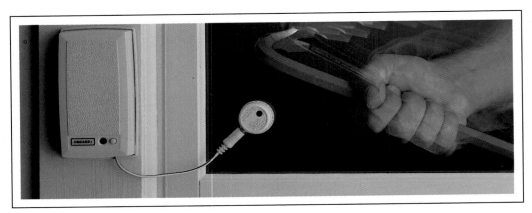

PRODUCT ADVANCES: ABOVE AND RIGHT, a long line of Amway security products for home, office, anywhere! OPPOSITE, LEFT AND BOTTOM RIGHT, the Amway Water Treatment System ... "pure and simple." OPPOSITE, TOP RIGHT, Glister Anti-Plaque Oral Rinse® and the Propulse Oral Delivery System®.

larger operations have almost the same degree of sophistication that we have here in the States," explains Van Andel, "but in some respects several are ahead of us in technology. In parts of France and the United Kingdom, for instance, the system makes it possible for customers to order right through their television sets."

The late seventies and early eighties brought further advances in the types and components of products offered under the Amway trademark. "It's interesting," says Van Andel, "how in one way we're back where we were many years ago in that we have some big-ticket items that are doing very well in the business today. Of course, one change from those years is the prevalence of the credit card. We couldn't

have done it 20 or 25 years ago, but now we can very easily sell items in the four-, five-, six-, and even seven-hundred-dollar range through credit cards, augmented by our consumer credit program. These bigger-ticket items make the business more profitable for the distributor — a very basic requirement.

"We're also finding that the more mundane household products are more difficult to base our marketing on today, even though they are an important, solid part of the business. You must have other products. That's why our cosmetics lines and the big-ticket perimeter alarms, water filters, and products of that kind are doing more than their share of driving the business."

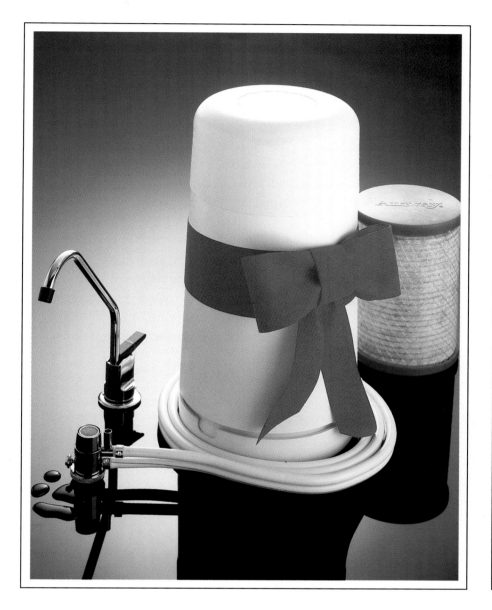

In 1982, after several years of producing cosmetics at Nutrilite's Buena Park plant (the company was acquired in 1972), increasing demand outpaced the manufacturing capacity to keep up with it. It was resolved to transfer the production of cosmetics to Ada, a decision that resulted in the construction of an ultramodern, three-level plant for that purpose, dedicated in January 1984. The plant, which produces almost 100 percent of the U.S. Artistry line, is a cross between a conventional cosmetics plant and a pharmaceutical laboratory. Extraordinary care is taken to prevent contamination and preserve the purity and high quality of the products. The plant has established industry standards for cleanliness and efficiency.

That same dedication to quality, at what management likes to refer to as the "100 percent level," is aptly demonstrated throughout today's distribution system. One of the basic safeguards is a section, common to every Amway distribution operation in the world, known as OSD — Overs, Shorts, and Damages. Realistically, it is almost impossible for any organization to ship merchandise in volume like this without sooner or later experiencing shortages, overages, or damages. Experience shows that when a thousand cases of goods are shipped, four or five errors will show up. But the new Amway system is so effective that it manages to reduce errors to one-fourth and even one-tenth of that level. During one month in the fall of 1983, Amway had two

distribution centers that were striving for absolute zero. And one of them made it!

Amway has never faltered in its dedication to the distributor or in its pledge to offer people a real opportunity to start their own business and prosper according to their drive and initiative. In the late 1970s and early 1980s, the emphasis had seemed to shift away from the importance of the *product* to the nature of the business itself. But a renewal of the early sense of devotion to product has taken place in the last two years.

It makes little difference in attitude that the lines and types of products change with the years. Distributors still have to base their degree of success on product sales. They still — perhaps even more than ever — have to cater to a buying public that thinks of Amway as the company that provides personal, one-to-one attention.

DID YOU KNOW ...

How well do Amway products sell? Consider these "Fun Facts":

- In one typical year, enough S-A-8 Laundry Detergent was sold to have washed a pile of clothes one mile high and covering 22 acres.
- If all the Artistry Cosmetics compacts alone that were sold in one year were opened and laid side by side, they would cover an area the size of three football fields.
- The amount of L.O.C. Cleaner sold in 1983 could clean a wall eight feet high, stretching to the moon and back five times.
- Enough Dish Drops Dishwashing Liquid was sold in 12 months to wash the dinner plate of every man, woman, and child in the world for one week.
- Enough Nutrilite Food Supplement tablets are sold each year to form a chain of tablets that could stretch from San Francisco to Shanghai, with 447 million tablets left over.
- In one year, Amway sells enough See Spray® Lens Cleaner to clean almost 150 million pairs of eyeglasses.

THE SKY'S NO LIMIT: LEFT, S-A-8 sales go out of sight. ABOVE, the Amway Personal Shoppers Catalog, a "dream book" with thousands of products.

Celebration and fireworks marking the Grand Opening of the Tower addition to the Amway Grand Plaza Hotel.

Chapter Seven

THE MARK OF LEADERSHIP

"A good leader inspires others with confidence in him; but a great leader inspires them with confidence in themselves."
— *Thomas Jefferson*

In a 1979 article, the *Grand Rapids Press* marveled at the machine that worked 24 hours a day without grumbling, executed instructions in billionths of a second, printed 2,000 lines per minute, and "talked" to its counterparts around the world. The machine in question was Amway's computer, the third generation of one that had been installed 12 years earlier to tackle the intricate record-keeping and communications needs of a rapidly expanding business. A company spokesman was quoted as revealing that it would take as many as ten thousand employees to do the work of this single computer. Without such technology, he said, keeping track of the company's growing force of more than 300,000 distributors would be close to impossible.

Symbolically, the computer was keeping pace with the company's development, highlighted by a major reorganization in the fall of 1970 that served to upgrade and streamline the entire corporate administrative structure. The blueprint called for Jay Van Andel and Rich DeVos to continue as chairman of the board and president respectively. But the daily administration was assigned to four new vice presidents who formed an Executive Committee, with the two founders serving as a Policy Committee to review all recommendations and proposals for new ventures.

Orville Hoxie was appointed to the new position of vice president of production and distribution; C. Dale Discher retained his office as corporate treasurer and assumed the title of vice president for finance; William Halliday became vice president for corporate services; and J. Austen Wood, vice president for corporate development and marketing. Acting as liaison between the Executive and Policy Committees was Gordon Teska, with the title of administrative assistant.

The reorganization spread outward from headquarters to the entire distribution system. A major change was the replacement of 30 regional warehouses with seven new regional distribution centers (RDCs) in Georgia, Michigan, Texas, California, New Jersey, Washington, and Colorado.

Under this greatly streamlined system, products could now be shipped from the Ada plant or from other manufacturers directly to the RDCs for processing. At each center, individual orders were filled on a weekly timetable and loaded aboard the trailers of contract haulers for delivery within their assigned network of distributors.

The communications system was improved at the same time, so that distributors promptly received all literature relating to new products, training programs, advertising, public relations, and general company news. Special programs were always conveyed in such a way that distributors could participate to the degree desired, or at the very least take pride in what the company was doing to enhance its name and stature. A good example was the opening of the Center of Free Enterprise, whose inaugural ceremony was attended by six thousand spectators and whose guest speaker was Gerald R. Ford, then a United States Congressman from Michigan.

Diversification and acquisition were two topics that were receiving more and more attention, as management explored new ways to improve and develop Amway still further. The acquisition program had really been kicked off in 1972 after a decision that was personally satisfying to Van Andel and DeVos. This was the purchase of Nutrilite Products, Inc., the company that had introduced them to direct selling in the first place.

The purchase of Nutrilite was a step into familiar territory, as well as an opportunity to acquire a product line that would fit well into distributor sales programs. By contrast, the acquisition of the Mutual Broadcasting Company in August 1977 was a venture onto unfamiliar ground. Yet it typifies the kind of commitment management was willing to make to achieve a more productive corporate entity. Mutual was noted for its news broadcasts and programming at 800 affiliated radio stations.

Three other significant acquisitions during Amway's second decade were motivated by the desire to provide further incentives and attractive meeting places for key distributors. The oceangoing motorship *Enterprise II* was purchased in 1972 to serve as a floating conference center for distributors whose sales and sponsorship achievements qualified them for entrance

into the Diamond Club. A luxury hotel/resort complex on Peter Island in the British Virgin Islands was purchased in 1978 to complement the seagoing facilities and motivate distributors to increase their sales and qualify for vacation-style meetings on location.

The third favorable acquisition was the Pantlind Hotel in Grand Rapids, the use of which would establish Amway's position as the region's largest user of meeting and lodging facilities. Although the hotel had fallen on hard times and was badly in need of renovation, it had once been a landmark in a city which thousands of furniture dealers visited regularly to place orders for Grand Rapids' best known product.

"We hadn't intended to become hotel owners," laughs DeVos, acknowledging that the company was active, however, in efforts to renew the city's decaying urban areas. "We backed into it. It started out simply as a recommendation to build a reasonably good hotel downtown. One thing led to another and we ended up making a major addition to the city."

Renamed the Amway Grand Plaza Hotel, with the subsequent construction of the adjoining Grand Plaza Tower, the complex is regarded as a world-class hotel, and is a source of great pride for the owners. "Jay and I and our wives," said DeVos at the opening ceremonies, "dedicate this hotel to the people of this community who, by their efforts, make this a great place to live. We pray that all who enter here may find the same love and warmth we have found."

ON THE MOVE: OPPOSITE, TOP, the launching of the oceangoing motorship Enterprise IV in August 1985. OPPOSITE, CENTER and BOTTOM, Amway's air fleet makes it easy for executives to attend key meetings and distributor rallies. ABOVE, aerial view of the factories and farmlands of Nutrilite Products, Inc., an Amway subsidiary since 1972. TOP RIGHT and BOTTOM RIGHT, Amway's fleet of trucks and railroad cars speed products to the distributor.

REVIVING A LANDMARK: OPPOSITE, TOP LEFT: *Monroe Street entrance to the Amway Grand Plaza Hotel.* OPPOSITE, TOP RIGHT, *DeVos, Van Andel, and former President Gerald R. Ford at ribbon-cutting ceremony.* OPPOSITE, CENTER LEFT, *Van Andel, Ford, and DeVos at the dedication gala.* OPPOSITE, BOTTOM LEFT, *Amway's owners inspect the artwork to be hung in the Amway Grand Plaza Hotel.* OPPOSITE, BOTTOM RIGHT, *celebrations at the dedication of the remodeled Amway Grand Plaza.* ABOVE, *two scenes from the festivities at the Amway Grand Plaza topping-off ceremony.* ABOVE, RIGHT, *Chairman Van Andel addresses distinguished guests at the Grand Plaza dedication ceremonies.* BELOW, *Amway's co-founders prepare to cement the hotel's cornerstone as wives Betty Van Andel and Helen DeVos look on.*

THE AMWAY CONCEPT IN ACTION

In its first ten years, Amway had expanded and multiplied its sales nearly 200 times over. The record was not one that was likely ever to be beaten. Yet other factors, perhaps not so dramatic, were contributing to a distinctive corporate maturity and stature. In the 1970s, Amway would reorganize its whole administrative structure, improve old products and add new ones after scientific research and thorough test marketing, select attractive sites for a continuing series of incentive seminars for distributors, diversify into new fields, and expand into overseas markets.

At the heart of this healthy growth was — and would continue to be — what was known as "the Amway philosophy, a way of life." This concept is rooted in the personal beliefs and convictions of the two founders, who have practiced what they preach in countless speeches and articles, during interviews with the press, and in the videotapes and audio cassettes available to distributors.

"I hope Amway does reflect what we believe," DeVos has said many times over. "The company is a reflection of us."

At the core of the Amway philosophy lies a strong belief in the virtues and benefits of free enterprise. Both DeVos and Van Andel have long maintained that this outlook has fostered their own success and must be preserved if future generations of businesspeople are to enjoy the same opportunities. Most importantly, the interpretation of the philosophy is a basic, down-to-earth one, not a stuffy and complex rehash of intellectual economic theories.

THE SHOW MUST GO ON: Undaunted by a driving rainstorm, Amway's owners preside over topping-off ceremonies for the Amway Grand Plaza Hotel.

"We recognized at the time we started Amway," says Van Andel, "that we were going to bring a lot of people into the business world as entrepreneurs who had never thought of doing this before. That is, of course, the basic concept of free enterprise. Our concept of it essentially wraps around the business of being an independent entrepreneur, running your own ship, so to speak. All of these things are what attract people into the Amway business to begin with, and we decided early on that our cause goes beyond that of a simple, materialistic way of making money.

"The free enterprise system does not revolve around the General Motors Corporations of this world. It revolves around the small-business system. There are at least 15 million small businesses in this country — gasoline stations, barber shops, hardware stores, grocery stores, bars, restaurants, and all those things — and basically these form the real core of the American free enterprise system. These small businesses are where it all starts, because every big business was once a small business, not something that dropped out of the sky full-blown."

DeVos reveals the same viewpoint. "Our involvement with free enterprise was really a step-by-step process. You know, we sat in the basement talking about the concept of Amway and the simple words came out that the idea of owning and operating our own business, of being rewarded in relationship to what we did, were just things we felt and believed in. We felt at the beginning that Amway needed to stand up for something, and the principles of free enterprise were the very foundations on which Amway was built.

"Amway distributors are constantly fostering and perpetuating this concept of free enterprise, whether they realize it or not. When they sponsor new distributors, they put them in business and make them active participants in the system. That step attracts more converts to the concept of free enterprise than all the talking and reading and lecturing will ever do. They rise or fall, but they gain a new respect for what it takes to make a business run."

From Amway's point of view, personal freedom springs from economic freedom. "Freedom and free enterprise are like Siamese twins," Van Andel once said. "One cannot live without the other. Allowing people the freedom to work for themselves and compete in a free marketplace has been the best, most productive economic approach ever devised."

Successful Amway distributors have echoed this outlook in their own personal comments for a quarter of a century now. "People must directly enter the free enterprise system to succeed," say Emerald Direct Distributors Moses and Audrey Burt of Virginia, "and the opportunity we now have with Amway provides the best opportunity to do that. Our greatest challenge is to succeed and show others that it can be done."

For Emerald Direct Distributors Earnest and Catherine Humphrey of Michigan, the free enterprise concept has "afforded us the opportunity to control our own destiny. The business allows us to have a full life, not just a life of mediocrity."

"We can be our own boss in Amway," say Double Diamonds Robb and Marilyn Tobey of Oregon. "We work extremely hard, but it's because we choose to do it — not because of some time clock. This freedom is very precious to us. It's what we want for our children. That's why the preservation of free enterprise and the Amway Sales and Marketing Plan are so important to us. It's not just the dollars; it's the quality of life that we've found. Being able to determine for ourselves what our life will be means so much to us. And we want our kids to have this same freedom."

Bill Britt was a city manager in North Carolina when he and his wife, Peggy, started their Amway business. Now as a very successful distributor at the Triple Diamond level, Bill has traded the narrow scope of city government for politics on a larger scale. He speaks widely on the subject of free enterprise and has served the conservative cause on various national issues.

ONLY THE BEST: Over highways and rail lines across America, the huge Amway distribution network comes down to this — the best products, delivered to the distributor with speed, precision, and care.

One of the exciting aspects of the Amway philosophy is that the free enterprise system, although we think of it as typically American, works in other countries as well. Consider this comment from distributors Edward and Patria Lourdes Silfa, working together in the Dominican Republic. "It's great to be the owners of our own business and learn the self-discipline that is required to develop it. What motivates us most in our Amway business is helping other people realize their own potential."

SELLING THE FREE ENTERPRISE SYSTEM

The company's management supports the laissez-faire doctrine, that is, one that opposes government intervention in business beyond the minimum necessary to protect personal and property rights. The founders of Amway have long opposed the flood of nit-picking regulations that stifle initiative and bloat the costs of doing business. "In our free enterprise economic system," explains DeVos, "the businessman owns his own tools, risks his own money, sets his own price, reaches his own decisions, and makes or loses money depending upon how well he provides the public with a product or service it wants at a price it is willing to pay. Unless he does something criminal or violates the public interest, the government should leave him alone."

Both Van Andel and DeVos are concerned that America seems to be moving away from free enterprise toward a socialistic system that increases government control over productivity. "The only alternative to free enterprise," they caution, "is socialism or, in its extreme form, communism. Free enterprise is more than mere economic theory. It is the economic dimension of liberty, an integral part of human freedom."

It is characteristic of the Amway philosophy as a way of life, and not simply the approach to a sales program, that this changing perspective prompted positive action. DeVos and Van Andel expressed alarm that economic instruction in schools was focusing much more on theory than on practice, and that students were seldom being taught that companies needed profits to pay salaries, expand, and even survive. Thus it was that they were motivated to create the Free Enterprise Institute. Physically, the institute started with an exhibit that had been used by the American Economic Foundation at the New York World's Fair to explain free enterprise to visitors from all over the world. The exhibit was transported to Ada

and installed in a section of the new headquarters building that was designated the Center of Free Enterprise.

Today, the Center greets visitors with reproductions of several of America's most telling economic and historical documents, including the Declaration of Independence, the Bill of Rights, and the Mayflower Compact.

Founded "to make people more aware of their responsibilities in a free society," the Institute reaches out to colleges, schools, community service groups, and interested citizens alike. It schedules speakers, conducts seminars, and provides a wealth of material, including training aids, books, and films, and a reference service, the Free Enterprise Resource Index.

The creation of the Institute and the Center occurred at about the time DeVos was committing important segments of his time and effort to reaching diverse audiences with a vital speech, "Selling America." He was discovering, to his surprise and gratification, that there were numerous listeners who were concerned about America's drift toward liberalism. Many sent him clippings and publications. Others expressed an eagerness to learn more about the subject. What it all boiled down to was that Amway became known as a company that cared about the freedom of the small businessperson and the preservation of America's traditional economic rights.

CLEAR SAILING: The Enterprise IV, floating conference center for Diamond Direct Distributors.

People — employees and distributors alike — have responded enthusiastically to the concept of free enterprise. One striking example of this kind of response by an Amway distributor is Freedom Run, in which contestants of different ages, backgrounds, and degrees of athletic prowess complete a six-mile course to raise funds for films which carry the message of freedom to people around the world. Some even race in wheelchairs, determined to cross the distant finish line and be rewarded with pledges from contributors.

The event was the brainchild of Cheri Jarrett-Brockman, a Double Diamond Direct Distributor from California, now living in Grand Rapids. This former physical education teacher says, "I decided to dedicate my time and energy to a large cause. I have a crazy mind. It's always flashing on new ideas. But I knew the Freedom Run concept was a good one — and it works!"

Her crusade began after she became familiar with the work of a nonprofit company that was producing educational films on such varied topics as drug addiction, child abuse, family life, and personal faith. Funds were needed to produce and distribute these films to audiences that would find inspiration in their messages. "One film can affect so many people," says Cheri, "that I felt Freedom Run, with its proceeds going to this cause, was a wonderful way to send positive messages to communities everywhere."

Cheri has organized more than one hundred Freedom Run races in the United States and Canada to salute freedom and the free enterprise system. One measure of the program's success is that it has received endorsements from many famous Americans, including First Lady Nancy Reagan, astronaut Sally Ride, sports figures Roger Staubach and Reggie Jackson, and Supreme Court Justice Sandra Day O'Connor.

The voice of free enterprise rings loud and clear in another way as Amway and its distributors commemorate Free Enterprise Day each year with huge rallies across the country. In January 1984, the company helped to sponsor a gigantic "Spirit of America — Free Enterprise" rally in Atlanta, Georgia, that was attended by thousands of people. The other hosts were the United States Chamber of Commerce, the Georgia Chamber of Commerce, and Citizen's Choice, a group that Van Andel had helped to organize to speak out against excessive government spending and regulation. Amway rented the auditorium, assigning volunteer distributors to hand out tickets and serve as ushers.

The experience was one that few of the participating distributors are soon likely to forget, as they all strive to preserve the free enterprise system.

Appropriately, Rich DeVos presented the keynote address, heralding free enterprise as "the spirit of America, which allows individuals who believe in themselves and their abilities, to achieve."

To Jay Van Andel went the honor of introducing featured speaker and eminent guest President Ronald Reagan.

"THE SPIRIT OF AMERICA": ABOVE, corporate and government dignitaries line the stage as President Ronald Reagan addresses the 1984 "Spirit of America — Free Enterprise" rally in Atlanta, Georgia. OPPOSITE, TOP LEFT, Amway's chairman takes the podium. OPPOSITE, TOP RIGHT, honored guest and featured speaker President Ronald Reagan. OPPOSITE, BOTTOM, thousands of free enterprise boosters signal their approval.

SPEAKING OUT: Amway Chairman Jay Van Andel speaking on tax reform before the Senate Finance Committee, June 1985.

MEETING CHALLENGES, MARCHING AHEAD

Free enterprise can be a sensitive, if not highly controversial, subject. Those who succeed under this system discover that success inevitably attracts scrutiny, and not always the beneficial kind. Almost since its founding Amway had endured accusations that it was fostering a "pyramid" scheme, whereby participants made their profits by signing up salespeople, with the newest recruits left holding the bag. Public concern grew as a number of fraudulent schemes were exposed and, in 1969, the Federal Trade Commission (FTC) began to investigate several companies, Amway and Nutrilite among them. Six years later, a formal complaint was issued to Amway.

Two more years passed as company attorneys wrestled with the FTC in efforts to determine what charges would be made, what depositions should be taken, what documents were required, and how to prepare for the forthcoming hearings.

The three-month-long hearings began in May 1977. Then, after nearly a year of deliberation, the administrative law judge rendered his decision: Most of the charges were dismissed. Equally important, the judge found, and the full Federal Trade Commission subsequently affirmed, that the Amway Sales and Marketing Plan was a legitimate multilevel sales opportunity and not, as had been charged, an illegal pyramid scheme. This landmark ruling cleared the air and made it possible for the company to continue its operations in the spirit of free enterprise that had characterized them since the beginning.

As the final years of the seventies drew to a close, Amway's management could point to a period of steady progress in which estimated retail sales had nearly trebled — from slightly more than $125 million in 1970 to almost $375 million in 1977. Over the next five years, the estimated retail sales would grow an average of $200 million a year, to reach a total of almost $1.5 *billion* in 1982.

Distributors in ever-greater numbers were scaling the Amway heights, looking to futures that were brighter and more promising than ever. Recruits were attracted by the undeniable evidence of dramatic sales growth. Amway's remarkable maturity as a major multinational corporation was enhanced by the enthusiastic enlistment of new distributors throughout the United States and Canada, the opening of international affiliates in Europe, Australia, and Asia, and the constant improvement of manufacturing facilities, products, and networks of distribution and communication. No longer was Amway referred to as the "direct-sales Michigan soap company." Its billion-dollar annual revenue, over seven thousand permanent employees, and more than one million distributors worldwide placed it among the 250 largest companies in the United States.

On the heels of this period of intensified growth came another major legal challenge. In November 1982, front page headlines in American and Canadian newspapers announced that the Canadian government was charging the Amway Corporation and Amway of Canada, Ltd., with failing to pay sufficient Canadian customs duties on goods imported into Canada from the United States.

Since 1965, Amway of Canada, Ltd., had been importing goods, but at transfer prices that it regarded as correct and authorized according to prior discussions and agreements with Canadian customs officials. However, Canadian officials now insisted that Amway should have valued these goods at the higher wholesale prices charged to U.S. distributors with no reduction in value for bonuses paid.

LEGAL CHALLENGE: At a press conference called by Amway, Van Andel clarifies the Canadian tax controversy.

In the fall of 1983, the matter was settled by the payment of substantial fines by both companies. Explaining Amway's position in a full-page advertisement in the *Wall Street Journal*, executive vice president and general counsel Otto Stolz stressed a significant point in this decision: "Jay Van Andel and Rich DeVos had a very strong legal basis for continuing to fight against Canadian authorities. In fact, none of the lawyers ever recommended that they settle. Their decision was clearly based on the overall best interests of the individuals within the Amway Corporation. They were willing to agree to the very stiff terms unilaterally demanded by the Canadians to avoid the divisions, frictions, and tensions that would have occurred if the litigation had continued."

The proceedings cast a temporary cloud over what had been considered one of the most exciting periods of Amway's history. Relieved by the termination of the lengthy, disruptive controversy, distributors were once again able to devote their full energies to the business at hand.

HARD WORK + GOOD JUDGMENT = SUCCESS

The Amway Corporation at the beginning of the 1980s was something of a contradiction, prospering at a time when the United States and many countries abroad were in the grip of an economic recession. How could this be? Van Andel explained to one incredulous interviewer that the company had *expected* continued growth during this period. "It has been our experience," he said, "that more people become Amway distributors during a recession. Our business has never been adversely affected by economic hard times."

That brand of brash confidence, combined with the outspokenness of the founders on the subject of free enterprise and in support of conservative political and social causes, was bound to attract attention from the press. One of the most interested commentators was Mike Wallace, famed for his bulldog style of interviewing on the CBS television program "60 Minutes." During a 1983 segment of the show, he aired films of distributor rallies and interviews with Amway's owners and distributors, successful and not-so-successful alike. His broadcast acknowledged that

UNTARNISHED IMAGE: OPPOSITE, TOP, Mike Wallace of CBS's 60 Minutes. OPPOSITE, CENTER, a light moment before the 60 Minutes interview. OPPOSITE, BOTTOM (left to right), Amway Public Relations Manager Jack Wilkie, Jay Van Andel, 60 Minutes Producer Alan Maraynes, Mike Wallace, Rich DeVos, Amway Director of Public Relations Casey Wondergem. ABOVE, TOP, an in-depth interview. ABOVE, BOTTOM, Wallace gets the distributor's point of view from Crown Direct Distributors Birdie and Dexter Yager. RIGHT, meeting the people in the field, at a Yager Distributor Rally.

"a strict code of ethics tells just how distributors should behave in the field, but because Amway's one million distributors are independent businessmen, Amway is powerless to control them."

The company, Wallace reported after thorough investigation, was "painting a realistic picture of just how much work it takes to succeed." In a later interview with Mutual Broadcasting's Larry King, Wallace conceded that he had actually started his editorial research on Amway with several "preconceived misconceptions," but that his attitude was now so positive that "this is going to sound like a commercial for Amway." Wallace, in fact, concluded that "their products are good" and that "the people in Ada are first-rate."

The "60 Minutes" episode typifies Amway's history of being frequently criticized for having a characteristic nonconformity and for being sometimes controversial and often aggressive in its marketing strategies. Typical, too, is the outcome, whereby the company has flourished under investigative pressure and preserved an untarnished image.

Disdaining traditional "How to Succeed in Business" blueprints, the two founders have preferred to follow their own gut feelings for getting ahead. "We have a company where two of us run it," DeVos once explained to a business journalist. "The entre-preneurial type usually isn't too well organized. You follow your leads and your instincts rather than massive, five-year planning charts .... There were times in the early days when we both had different ideas. Gradually, as we evaluated our ideas and individual reactions, we distilled the policies, principles, and concepts by which we work."

"You store up all of what you have learned before, " concurs Van Andel, "and that is called *judgment*."

Because of, rather than in spite of, the difference in approach, the judgment has paid off handsomely.

After a quarter of a century, the company built on their principles remains one of the classic success stories of our times. That is not to say that Amway's growth has never encountered a dip or slide. The curves of growth and profits show the kinds of variations that make the picture real and believable. But the general trend has been steadily upward and healthy. The factors that contribute to success are the only elements that seem to remain unchanging. The business environment, both at home and abroad, still encourages individual initiative, and countless hundreds of thousands still seek the kind of future Amway offers.

"We know today," says Van Andel confidently, "that there will always be a new group of individuals coming along tomorrow, looking for a chance to do their own thing. And we want to be there, offering that opportunity."

A QUARTER-CENTURY AND GROWING:
OPPOSITE, 60 Minutes' *Mike Wallace discusses his preconceptions and impressions of Amway in an interview with Mutual Broadcasting's Larry King. ABOVE, TOP, sunset on the eternal flame sculpture outside the Center of Free Enterprise. ABOVE, BOTTOM, an impressive milestone, $1 billion in sales. LEFT, Amway's Ada complex today.*

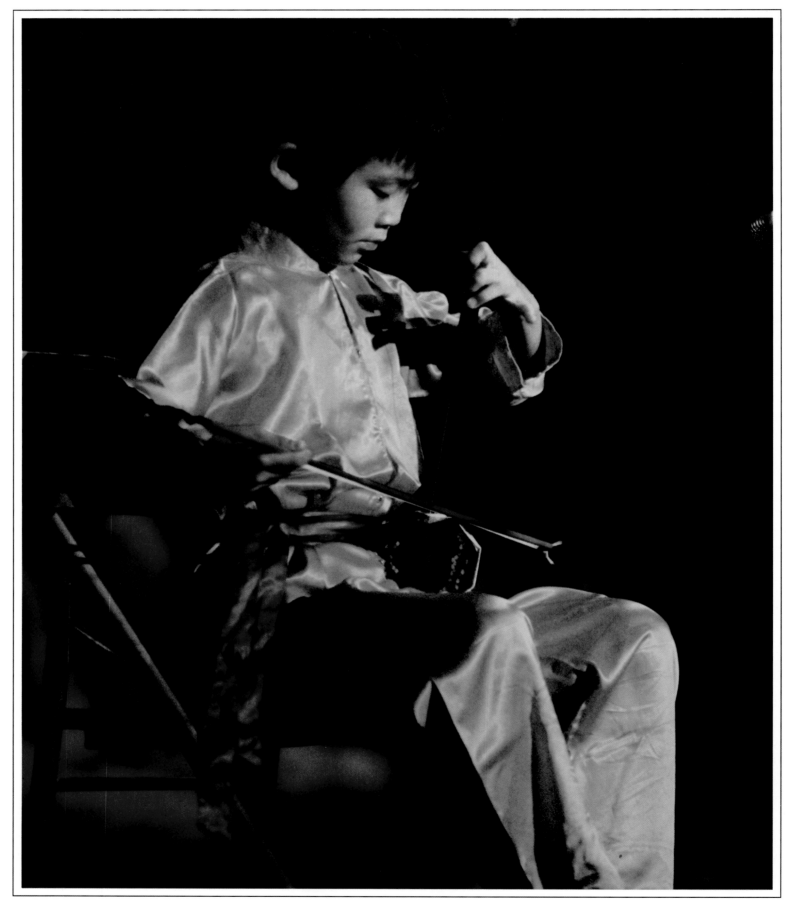

A thoughtful performance on the ancient erdu, during the 1983 Amway-sponsored American tour of the Hong Kong Children's Choir.

Chapter Eight

MEETING WORLD MARKET NEEDS

"When you look at the world in a narrow way, how narrow it seems! ... When you look at it selfishly, how selfish it is! But when you look at it in a broad, generous, friendly spirit, what wonderful people you then find in it!"
— *Horace Rutledge*

Apart from the record sales, the rapid expansion of the company, and the tens of thousands of people who have swelled the ranks during the last two and a half decades, there is something even more astonishing about Amway than can be found in the corporate facts and figures. This unique surprise is that the Amway philosophy that worked in two makeshift basement offices in Middle America is gloriously successful, not just in one town or one state or one country, but around the world.

The distinguished British novelist of the nineteenth century, William Makepeace Thackeray, once wrote that the world was a looking glass that gave back to all persons the reflection of their own faces. People had the power to interpret the world in their own image, no matter where they happened to live. The history of Amway has proven the truth of Thackeray's perception, demonstrating again and again that individuals can control their destinies to a great extent by their attitudes and outlooks, as well as by their actions.

What works in Keokuk, Iowa; Friendship, Maine; and Love, Texas can also work in Fremantle, Australia; Kawasaki, Japan; and Llanfairfechan, Wales.

It requires considerable imagination to picture the walls of the Van Andel and DeVos basements that defined the world of Amway less than three decades ago and see this cramped space magically expanding into facilities serving some 40 countries and territories. Yet it does not stretch credulity quite so much to picture circles of people reaching out to more and more circles of people until eventually their legions encompass the globe. The people-to-people image, by contrast to the image of physical expansion, is more like an arithmetical progression. Yet the numbers are secondary to the philosophy and concept that nurtured the growth and made it possible.

"The entrepreneurial spirit seems to be in everybody, everywhere," says DeVos when trying to explain how it was possible for Amway International to establish 11 foreign affiliates in as many years. "What Amway does is provide the opportunity."

The overseas potential first became apparent when, in 1965, Jay Van Andel was invited to be one of 70 trade delegates to explore opportunities abroad. The purpose of the delegation, formed by then Michigan Governor George Romney, was to establish trade contacts between Michigan and Western Europe. Although Van Andel became convinced that foreign soil was fertile ground, he and his partner decided to defer overseas expansion in favor of devoting full time to their vigorous North American operations.

They failed to reckon with eager distributors who also realized the potential on the other side of the Atlantic.

After Amway of Canada had been established in 1962 as an extension of the company's domestic operations, it had quickly and effectively proved that the philosophy and the Sales and Marketing Plan could be successfully "exported." Getting wind of the fact that management was at least exploring the idea of overseas operations, distributors began deluging headquarters with requests for overseas sponsoring information. Prompted by the brimming interest and the sheer numbers of the would-be foreign entrepreneurs, DeVos and Van Andel began to survey

and study possible international markets. By 1969, they had fixed their sights firmly on Australia.

Although the choice was termed "unscientific" and made without intensive market research, Australia was selected for its cultural and economic similarity to the United States. A more telling reason, supported by the Marketing Division, was that the Amway Sales and Marketing Plan and the concept of person-to-person selling would "prove irresistible to the enterprising Australians."

"We like the spirit of the people," DeVos explained at the time. "They are looking for opportunities; they have real faith in their country and in themselves; and they believe in the future. They're gung ho, and Amway's going to give them the opportunity to make it."

"An interesting thing in being here in Australia," says Peter Javelin, who with his wife Penny is a Triple Diamond Direct Distributor, "is that the national symbol, the kangaroo, doesn't jump backwards. It often stays still and looks around and surveys other perspectives.

"My wife and I learned from the school of hard knocks before we started in Amway. We had a paint factory, a business we fell into and couldn't seem to get out of. Finally we sold it and got into electrical appliances, gas installations — and you name it. We started sales teams and we made money and we invested in various stocks because we heard you had to speculate to accumulate. We believed it, but we ended up broke. That means 'bust' in every business or investment we got involved with — about ten of them.

"Well, like the kangaroo, to start moving forward you've got to take the big jump. And that's what we did, into Amway. And we're very excited about what we've seen and heard about what's happening in Australia and around the world of Amway. It's excitement. It's enthusiasm. It's motivation for the dream that can come true."

Bill Hemmer, today vice president for international operations support, spent nine months in Ada, Michigan, laying the groundwork for the new operation and another nine months in Sydney, Australia, setting the plans in motion. "Establishing a business in a foreign country," says Hemmer,

"THE BIG JUMP": ABOVE, *Amway of Australia corporate headquarters at Castle Hill, Sydney, Australia.* TOP RIGHT, *Amway of Canada, Ltd., complex, London, Ontario, Canada.* CENTER, *Laurie Mulham (right), then head of Amway of Australia, tours the Ada complex in 1972, with Bill Hemmer of Amway International Marketing as guide.* BELOW, *first visit to Ada of an Australian distributors group, 1975.*

"involves far more than just opening an office." For a time, he played one-man band, working with Sydney lawyers and accountants to make sure plans conformed to Australian laws, developing an appropriate product line, lining up distributors, explaining the plan, designing literature, and recruiting an Australian to head the new company.

Soon after it opened in April 1971, the new operation began attracting attention in the American, as well as the Australian, press. *Business Abroad* magazine reported in its July issue that Amway's "entrepreneurial gospel has been spreading like wildfire among Australian housewives and their husbands. Five nights a week groups of 150 to 250 cheering and clapping Australians have been assembling to listen to the message Amway Corporation has just exported from the U.S. — how to make a better-than-average living through sales."

The editors concluded that "anyone who has faced up to even a few minutes' worth of Amway President Richard DeVos's free enterprise evangelism is likely to give odds that his company will score high on its first overseas venture."

"THE WORLD'S OUR OYSTER"

Hemmer and Laurence Mulham, who had been selected as Amway Australia's first chief executives, signed up about 400 distributors during their first month of operation and soon afterward were reporting their first Direct Distributors. But the business didn't skyrocket as expected. "It started nicely," explains Hemmer, "then it slowed down and stayed there."

There was no problem with the Amway concept itself or the vigorous enthusiasm of the participants Down Under. Rather, it lay with the product line. Amway had contracted with Australian vendors to manufacture all products to its exacting specifications. But quality control proved to be a major weakness, along with erratic production and supply. For a time the situation looked bleak.

But the Australian experience proved to be the proverbial blessing in disguise.

"We found that we could ship the products from the United States cheaper than we could make them in Australia," Hemmer points out. This procedure solved the problems, both of quality and supply. More importantly, it also established the precedent whereby most overseas markets are supplied today by American-made products that are exported to the foreign distribution centers.

This practice, adds Van Andel, "keeps the business in our own plants where there is profit-making potential, creates local employment, improves the national balance of trade, and maximizes our quality control."

After its initial struggles, which continued into the second year of its existence, Amway Australia suddenly came to life. Responsible for the rejuvenation were the supply reorganization plan, the infusion of

EUROPEAN ENTERPRISE: *ABOVE, Amway's warehouse complex in the Netherlands. OPPOSITE, TOP LEFT, the original headquarters for Amway of Switzerland. OPPOSITE, TOP RIGHT, a modern Regional Distribution Center in France. OPPOSITE, CENTER LEFT, Stewart McArthur, then head of Amway (U.K.), Ltd., at the 1982 Amway U.K. National Convention. OPPOSITE, BOTTOM LEFT, one member of the Amway U.K. delivery fleet. OPPOSITE, BOTTOM RIGHT, Amway of France headquarters today.*

new products, including a cosmetics line, and the maturing of the fledgling distributor network. Sales doubled during one significant month and after that the business really took off. A year-end *Amagram* magazine jubilantly went on record with the report that Amway Australia had "turned the corner and is now achieving the kind of growth that is uniquely Amway."

That healthy spiral of growth has never slackened. The first Diamond (and then Double Diamond) Direct Distributors were Peter and Penny Javelin, announced in 1975, while the first Crown Directs were David and Nadia Comyns, in 1978.

The Comyns started in business part-time and with no security, David facing hostility in the jewelry store where he worked and Nadia coping with a shyness acquired as the child of immigrant Russian parents.

Just when they were beginning to be successful with Amway, David was temporarily paralyzed by the reappearance of an old injury suffered in an accident.

"Our job security reverted to zero," recalls Nadia, but they found that their income from Amway was more than their joint incomes from their regular work. When David recovered, he gave up his job and focused on Amway completely, followed a year later by his wife. They persevered and prospered. "We believe we've been successful," says David, "because we have adhered to the basics — basics that produce big personal group volume and strong, well-trained leaders who are capable of developing and guiding their own organizations."

GLOBAL AMBASSADORS: TOP LEFT, the headquarters of Amway's West German affiliate. TOP RIGHT, a group of French distributors visits Ada. BOTTOM LEFT, scene from the 1979 Amway U.K. National Distributors Convention. BOTTOM RIGHT, inside the West German Board Room.

The success of the "Australian Experiment" motivated Amway to launch a string of overseas affiliates in Western European countries where free enterprise permitted the proper functioning of the Sales and Marketing Plan. As had been the case with Australia, these European markets were selected on the basis of each country's economic and cultural compatibility with the United States. Over a period of seven years, six European affiliates were established, all wholly owned, independent enterprises. They included the United Kingdom and the Republic of Ireland in 1973, West Germany in 1975, France in 1977, the Netherlands in 1978, and Belgium and Switzerland in 1980. The history of each is fundamentally the same: growing sales, increasing numbers of sponsored distributors, and continuing records of achievements.

This brand of proven success eventually evoked a big question: Would the Amway concept also work successfully in Asian and Eastern cultures?

Opinions were divided. For everyone who thought the potential was promising there were others who could not conceive of the oriental life-style as one compatible with this kind of direct selling. Would Japanese women, for example, have the kind of social freedom needed to function as independent entrepreneurs? Would the kinds of products designed for western households appeal as well to oriental families?

"UNIQUELY AMWAY": TOP LEFT, a capacity crowd at Amway U.K.'s 1982 National Convention. TOP RIGHT, headquarters for Amway U.K. BOTTOM LEFT, Crown Direct Distributor Bernice Hansen speaks at Amway U.K.'s 1982 Convention. BOTTOM RIGHT, Grand Opening of the Amway Belgium headquarters, June 1983.

"Amway is basically a business opportunity," argued Al Meder, international marketing vice president until 1984. "It's that opportunity that people grasp for and there's demand for it anywhere you go in the world."

Hong Kong was selected for the first affiliate in the Far East, in part because many of its citizens were already familiar with American business procedures and products. After a slow start in the mid-1970s, sales began to increase steadily and, in some cases, dramatically. The expansion of facilities made it possible for Diamond and Double Diamond Distributors to emerge from the ranks.

The Hong Kong experiment led Amway down through the South China Sea to Malaysia, whose people seemed eager to have this kind of opportunity. The premise proved to be right. After Amway Malaysia was formed in 1976, it became one of the company's most successful markets, based on per capita income and population. One year after it was started, the affiliate experienced the fastest growth rate of any overseas operation up until that time and within three more years was quadrupling its annual sales figure.

If Malaysia had been a welcome surprise, Taiwan was even more so. Established in 1982, Amway Taiwan exceeded all forecasts in its first 18 months and continued to grow more rapidly than any previous overseas market.

PEOPLE ... PEOPLE ... PEOPLE

There is an old story whose origins are obscure, but which undoubtedly has been retold from generation to generation, since antiquity, in numerous versions. A wise man was asked by his prince why some of the people in his domain prospered while others, with seemingly equal opportunities, failed. By way of answering, the wise man selected three of the prince's subjects, a general, a mason, and a farmer, and escorted them to a barren plain not far from the castle.

"What is this land worth?" he asked each in turn, as the prince listened.

"Nothing," spat the soldier in disgust. "There is no town or rich mines to seize. I could not inspire my troops to risk their lives in battle over this flat stretch of ground."

EAST MEETS WEST: OPPOSITE, TOP, inside the new Amway Malaysia offices. OPPOSITE, CENTER, the Van Andels join in the celebration at the Grand Opening of Amway Hong Kong. OPPOSITE, BOTTOM, exotic sights at the 1982 Leadership Seminar in Malaysia. ABOVE,TOP, Amway Malaysia welcomes visitors Rich and Helen DeVos. ABOVE, BOTTOM LEFT, new Diamond Direct Distributor Chan Koon Tin, 1982. RIGHT, original headquarters for Amway Malaysia.

"Absolutely worthless," replied the mason, shaking his head. "I don't see a rock in sight which I could use for building even the simplest of huts."

"It is priceless!" exclaimed the farmer, "so much, much greater than my humble little vegetable plot. Why I see this in only a year as a vast field of golden grain!"

The moral of the story, of course, is that some people are excited and motivated by the opportunity they see, while others are too shortsighted to recognize the potential of something placed clearly in focus for them. The Malaysians, along with numerous other peoples on the other side of the oceans, are like the fabled farmer. There lies before them the promise of so much more than they have ever had, or dreamed of having.

Amway executives have experienced firsthand the superior motivation that leads people in developing nations to reach for opportunities to better themselves and their lives. This same motivation occurs among people who are displaced or who have gone through traumatic experiences that have critically disrupted their lives.

Consider, for example, the inspirational story of distributors Soua and May Yi Her. Citizens of Laos in Southeast Asia, they were victims of the civil strife that ripped the country apart in the 1960s and the plague of communism that began to stifle it in the mid-1970s. Targeted for elimination by the communists, they and a few others in their village were fortunate enough to escape to America in 1977.

"When we first arrived in this country seven years ago," recounts Soua, "neither May Yi nor I spoke any English. As you can imagine, we had to make many adjustments. The fast-paced American life-style was difficult for us to understand. We were determined to master the language and adapt to the culture. We love Laos, but political conditions made it impossible to return there."

The challenges and difficulties were many as they tried to make ends meet, at one time living in a low-rent apartment in Wisconsin inhabited by all kinds of seamy characters engaged in drugs and other illegal activities. The Hers were qualified for very few jobs, even though May Yi spent long hours studying at a local business school. Hearing about Amway by accident, they snapped up the opportunity to upgrade their living conditions.

"May Yi and I had looked into opening our own grocery store," says Soua, "but the costs were prohibitive. We'd been approached about Amway before, but no one had ever told us the entire Amway Sales and Marketing Plan. The right approach makes all the difference!"

They started out with the decision to include some of their friends and family in the business — most of them Laotians who had also escaped the communist net and fled to America. With the help of their sponsors, they presented the Amway concept, often serving as translators for those in the group who had not yet learned much English. As the group grew and split into other groups, explains Soua, "we eventually got other people to translate at our meetings. They were so excited after listening to the Plan and translating it for others, they were often the first to join."

"WE'VE COME SO FAR": Soua and May Yi Her make the transition from a life of poverty and despair to one of comfort and hope, thanks to the Amway opportunity.

The Hers travel all over Wisconsin working their Amway business and, through contacts in other states, have sponsored people all across the country. They not only translate product information, but even send out newsletters in their native tongue.

"We look forward to the future with optimism," says Soua. "We've come so very far. Amway has enabled us to help other people as well as ourselves — and it's helping us shape our future."

This same kind of spirit is duplicated in many countries abroad, proving that language and cultural barriers are relatively insignificant in comparison with the motivation and will to succeed. Japan, which in 1979 became Amway's fourth Asian affiliate, is a good example. Although economically developed and long engaged in trade with the United States, Japan presents more cultural differences than perhaps any other society in which Amway does business. The formidable language barrier, singular customs, and inflexible traditions have created occasional embarrassments and misinterpretations of the manner in which Amway business should be conducted. Even deliveries to distributors pose a challenge, since houses and streets are often numbered inconsistently and confusingly. Nevertheless, Amway of Japan — like its neighboring Eastern affiliates — has overcome these peculiarities to register ever-increasing sales year after year.

THE PROMISE OF MORE: ABOVE, TOP, New Direct Distributors Seminar, Hong Kong, 1982. ABOVE, BOTTOM, Rich DeVos speaks to Amway's Hong Kong distributors. RIGHT, corporate headquarters for Amway of Japan.

THE FAR-FLUNG AMWAY OPPORTUNITY

Would you like to have your own independent business at home, yet on an *international* scale?

Making this kind of objective possible documents one of the underlying keys to Amway's success. This kind of magic also demonstrates how vital people are in the warp and woof of what Amway has woven into its mantle of prosperity. The system of sponsoring distributors makes it possible for individuals to expand their businesses abroad, as well as at home. The sponsoring distributors receive a three percent bonus based on the business volume they stimulate through Direct Distributors in other countries. This kind of sponsorship, which also counts toward pin awards, is essential, says Bill Hemmer, because it helps to strengthen overseas networks. "It isn't the corporation that sponsors and develops distributors, although we work with them, supply the product, and provide guidance. As for the success of each market abroad, it all depends on the people in each country to achieve results."

The value of this people-to-people concept can be seen in many ways, not the least of which has been the manner in which the international business has spread and prospered. Experience has shown that floods of inquiries are always triggered by proposals to establish new overseas affiliates. This is followed by the efforts of people already with existing affiliates to help set up the new ones. Amway's Malaysian market was developed more effectively, for example, by sponsors in the earlier established Australian affiliate. In turn, much of the success of Amway Taiwan can be traced back to the efforts of enterprising Malaysian distributors.

The normal timetable for launching a foreign affiliate includes an initial period of 12 to 18 months to consolidate planning, train a basic staff, translate literature, lay the legal foundation, and register the company with local agencies and officials. Long before getting to this stage, however, Amway's management will have applied its strict benchmarks to the selection of the country or territory itself. Amway will not consider any locale unless the laws and regulations permit the establishment of a wholly owned corporation, the pursuit of free enterprise, and the freedom to operate, without significant modification, its Sales and Marketing Plan.

Taking into consideration the aforementioned outlay of time and capital, and the fact that sales and sponsoring in most markets start out small, DeVos cautions that "it may take years to generate enough volume to break even." He prefers to maintain a conservative outlook, despite some of the remarkable sales records that were achieved in as little as three and four years after first launching the overseas operations in the mid-1970s.

A sociology student researching international cultures could benefit immensely from studying Amway's inventories for its overseas affiliates. The facts and figures reveal a great deal about the people who live in foreign countries and regions.

PEOPLE-TO-PEOPLE: OPPOSITE, the international face of Amway. TOP LEFT, Rich DeVos greets new Direct Distributors in Germany. TOP RIGHT, Amway U.K. distributors applaud their own, at the 1982 National Convention. CENTER, distributors from Amway Netherlands join in a 1983 biking event. BOTTOM LEFT, Jay Van Andel addresses distributors in Hong Kong. BOTTOM RIGHT, a musical message at the 1978 Amway U.K. National Convention.

GLOBAL MARKETPLACE: TOP LEFT, products on their way to the distributor from Amway U.K.'s warehouse. TOP RIGHT, an international shipment. BOTTOM LEFT, products are adapted to suit the local language and culture. BOTTOM RIGHT, office personnel at Amway of Japan. OPPOSITE, a chance to share ideas and examine new products at Amway of Japan's 1982 National Convention.

Every month, distribution managers study product needs in Amway locations around the world. They keep track of each affiliate's inventory and watch its sales grow. From that information, they determine ahead of time what products are going to be needed, then manufacture and ship them accordingly. The popularity of products, country by country, reveals a great deal about the consumers who order and use them.

Not only do the products have to be selected according to local needs and preferences, but the packaging must be tastefully adapted to the dictates of the culture, while still retaining the Amway identity. Standard sizing may vary, as in the case of countries that traditionally use the metric system. The labels must carry product information in the language spoken by the intended consumers, as well as often in one or two other languages required by law or custom.

Beyond the mere fundamentals of shipment, such as booking the appropriate carriers and arranging for customs declarations and other paperwork, lie some critical and often sensitive requirements. Consider, for example, what could happen to products being transported through tropical regions where the temperatures inside containers often exceed 120°F. Imagine the severe vibrations that afflict products being trucked to the outback of Australia on rutted, gravelly roads. Or picture what might happen to a shipment of Nutrilite foodstuffs en route to the interior of Borneo by riverboat, where insect pests and humidity could quickly destroy perishable products that are not properly refrigerated and sealed.

While the full range of Amway products is not commonly distributed to international markets, at least 15 of the top 20 lines are available worldwide. These include Artistry Cosmetics, popular among peoples all over the globe. The best-sellers, however, have included some interesting surprises. Nutrilite Food Supplements are popular throughout Asia,

particularly in Malaysia where health is a constant preoccupation. Queen Cookware is also widely regarded in Asia and, in fact, throughout international markets, which account for about 60 percent of the line's total sales.

How is it possible that Amway products, which seem so specifically designed for American tastes and conditions, can go to market abroad just the way they are, with no changes except in packaging?

The answer to this question is that not all of them can, though a surprising number are the same from one country to another. Certain products must be custom-formulated for the environments in which they are to be used. Laundry compounds have to be modified, for example, for use in Malaysia where many women wash clothes in cool river water or (at the opposite end of the scale) for Europe, where the conventional washing machine heats its water to the boiling point. Insect sprays bound for Australia have to be specially formulated to counterattack the unique

species of household pests that live there. For the Japanese market, Amway has modified its line of skin-care products to take into consideration the fact that the users' complexions are more sensitive than those of their American counterparts.

The challenge of working in many culturally diverse and geographically far-flung world markets has greatly heightened the insight of the Amway executives who are concerned with international operations. "Thousands of Amway distributors around the world have been able to broaden their knowledge and enjoyment of the world at large," said Van Andel, "and at the same time increase their income and security."

The unique Amway Sales and Marketing Plan crosses a remarkable range of ideological, as well as economic, borders. DeVos likes to tell about the time he attended an international meeting and was introduced to an Amway distributor who turned out to be a French communist.

"How do you reconcile your communist convictions with your capitalistic business?" he asked.

The communist minced no words. "I need the money," he replied laconically.

Van Andel, referring to Amway's continuing program to meet the challenges of new business abroad in the future, says with conviction, "We'll be accomplishing something very worthwhile, promulgating the American system of free enterprise in areas where it is not normally done, or where it has been difficult in the past to open doors.

"That has been Amway's message and mission from the beginning: to provide an independent business opportunity to people in other lands, many of whom never thought such an opportunity would be open to them."

To prove the point, he need only let successful foreign distributors speak for themselves — Michael and Gaby Strachowitz of West Germany, for example. Starting in a small way with Amway in 1977, they became Crown Direct Distributors less than six years later. They are now Crown Ambassadors. "It's one thing to react with spontaneous enthusiasm to an idea," says Michael, speaking of their original excitement about their new work, "but it's quite another matter to stick to the idea and pursue it in a consistent, persistent way."

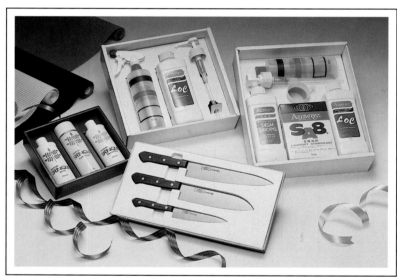

INTERNATIONAL EXCELLENCE: An assortment of popular Amway products from various countries proves that quality speaks a universal language.

"The secret to growth in this business," adds Gaby, "is persistence, a sense of responsibility for ourselves and others, and the courage to think big and act accordingly."

Characteristically, they reflect the same charismatic experience of Amway people all over the world. "Nowhere else would we have found so many friends as in the Amway business. Amway has also given us the opportunity we'd dreamed of so often — to be able to work together for personal and financial

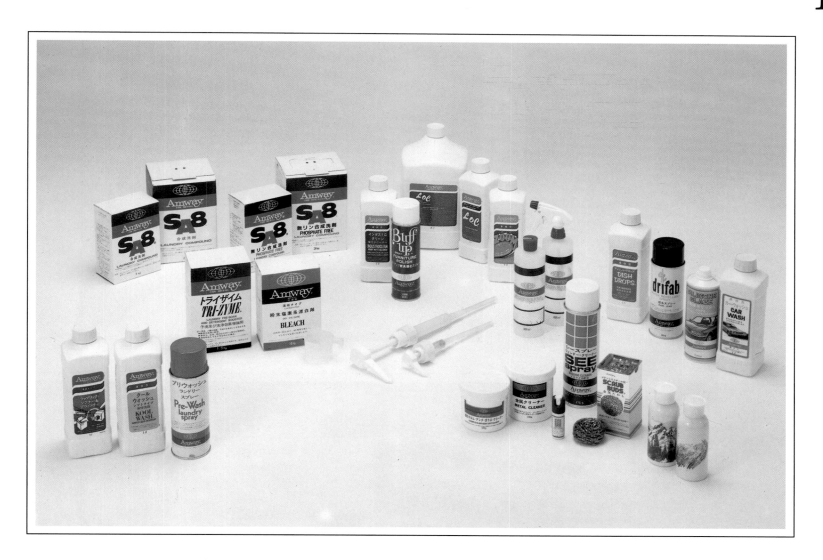

independence, to be free to organize our lives and work responsibilities as we please, and to be able to strive for self-realization. Even though it is really nice to experience personal success, our greatest pleasure comes from the success of our distributors."

The same spirit is echoed in France, with Joe and France Mas and their two children (in their twenties) who are also distributors. "What has really pleased us about Amway," comments Joe, who gave up good jobs in accounting and marketing in the United States to return to his native country, "is the fact of being able to work together and, in the end, to have a *life* together. Before Amway, we did not have a life. We each went our own way."

"When people first start working together as a couple," adds France, "there is often friction because each is used to working in his or her own way. But as you learn to appreciate each other, the talents of each, you find you can't work separately, and you love each other more. For us, this has been a constant honeymoon."

Having achieved the goal of Crown Ambassadors, the Mases' greatest thrill has been working with others. "During a period of three months," France says, "we sponsored 14 new distributors, and what is really exciting is that we tripled our personal volume during that period. We count on good planning and effective organization of the work, good work habits, personal sponsoring, and, especially, constant communication."

"Amway is like the sunrise," says France with her bright smile. "It visits all the houses if their windows are open."

It is fitting that in France, like so many other lands where Amway has ventured, there are a lot of open windows.

Scenes from the 1985 Amway Distributors Convention in Grand Rapids, Michigan. TOP LEFT, Helen and Rich DeVos. TOP RIGHT, Jay and Betty Van Andel.

Chapter Nine

THE AMWAY HERITAGE

"Today is yesterday's pupil."
— Benjamin Franklin

The great American industrialist Henry Kaiser, who participated in such momentous events as the building of the Hoover Dam, the construction of the San Francisco-Oakland Bridge, and the production of ships, planes, and military vehicles during World War II, had a direct answer for people who asked how he had achieved such historic success. "The simple word *faith*," he replied, "sums up what I am convinced makes the difference between attaining or not attaining the greatest values in life."

His concept of a fully rounded faith consisted of three parts: "Faith in yourself and your highest aspirations, which releases your creative inner powers and gives your daily life direction, adventure, and meaning; Faith in your fellow men whom you love and serve; and Faith in God that answers the questions and longings of your soul, gives you help from the Higher Source, and sees the work of the Creator in everything."

If there is one value that is constant in the Amway concept of living and working, it is certainly faith. From the day Jay Van Andel and Rich DeVos first conceived of a business requiring the coordinated efforts and enthusiastic response of multitudes of people working together, they themselves possessed this quality and expected it in all others who expected to achieve success. In an organization where *people* count most, this is a quality that builds and spreads with the addition of each new participant.

Nowhere has this brand of loyalty and singlemindedness been more dramatically evident than in the heritage of second- and even third-generation Amway distributors who have followed in the footsteps of their parents and joined the Amway family. The Delisles, introduced earlier, certainly personify this trend, representing three generations and four distributorships, all within the same family. In addition, they can point to what is increasingly common among Amway families: young children who are growing up in the same life-style and performing little assignments in their own way to help their parents in the business.

Characteristic of the "family" concept and heritage are Reuben and Lorraine Seagren, their oldest son, Lowell, and his wife Jennifer, who are all active distributors. "We've been in Amway since 1959," said Reuben on the occasion of the company's first quarter century, "and it's been an exciting 25 years — the most exciting years of our lives!"

Despite their record of achievement and their ever-increasing income, the Seagrens choose to reside in the same home in Rockford, Illinois, where they lived when they first joined Amway, and in which they brought up their two sons.

The Seagrens, Diamond Direct Distributors, attribute much of their long-term success to faith and commitment. "We're so enthused about the business that it carries over into everything we do," says Reuben. "I often laugh and say I might forget about my wife, but I always have Amway on my mind. The first thing I do in the morning is to ask myself, 'What am I going to do in the Amway business today?' I try to get others to feel the same way. You just have to forget any negatives, think positive, and have faith in yourself. Anyone can succeed who really has that kind of faith."

Supporting Reuben and Lorraine's philosophy of faith is the joy they derive from helping others to reach out and achieve their goals. "We spend most of our time with our immediate group," says Lorraine. "We set aside every Tuesday for our distributors. That is our product pick-up day and we use it regularly to demonstrate the lines, spread good news, and cheer our people on. Saturdays are set aside for long-distance calling, since we like to keep in close touch with distributors in Denver, Memphis, and Houston. Once our distributors become Directs, we step back and let them lead."

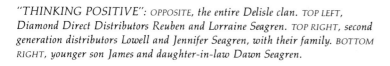

"THINKING POSITIVE": OPPOSITE, the entire Delisle clan. TOP LEFT, Diamond Direct Distributors Reuben and Lorraine Seagren. TOP RIGHT, second generation distributors Lowell and Jennifer Seagren, with their family. BOTTOM RIGHT, younger son James and daughter-in-law Dawn Seagren.

Summer always offers a bouquet of vivid colors around the Seagren home since Reuben is dedicated to his lush flower garden, which displays 85 rose and chrysanthemum bushes. "I'm a reader, myself," explains Lorraine, "but I get out with Reuben every morning for a one-mile walk, and we try to get in another walk each evening. It's so relaxing that our neighbors have started walking with us."

When the gusty midwestern winters blow, the Seagrens find time to escape to Arizona for a visit with their younger son, Jim.

"No matter what we do," says Lorraine, "Amway is part of our lives. We really never feel as though we're working. We're having fun. Sure, Reuben and I are busy, but it's so enjoyable that we don't consider it work."

One of the reasons is that there is no pressure. "In all the years that we have been in business," Reuben explains, "we have never asked anyone to buy Amway products. We just show people how great the products are and people want to buy them."

The Seagrens are delighted that their son Lowell and his wife, Jennifer, have become part of the Amway heritage and are now active distributors. Keeping the business in the family is a favorable sign that the Amway life-style is one that attracts every generation.

PARTNERS IN PROGRESS

In an attractive California suburb, the Amway heritage was highlighted in the early 1980s when the television camera focused on John and Pat Hendrickson. It was the occasion of their Crown Ambassador Day, the event that recognizes the highest level of achievement in the world of Amway. Six of the Amway distributors sharing their moment of recognition were very special: members of the Hendrickson family. Their oldest daughter, Jo Ann, was a biologist in heart research and a Direct Distributor; David, then 25, was also a Direct, with a degree in business management; Jill and her husband, Pete Borton, were Directs; Mary, then 20, was a Direct and an employee of a local bank; and the youngest daughter, Susan, though only 16 and a high-school student, had already become a distributor.

The decision to join Amway was made jointly by John and Pat in 1965, when it became apparent that the real estate business that had brought the family to California was on the skids. Since then, their fortunes have continued to rise and they have brought into Amway many distributors who had similar problems and needed real turning points in their lives. Many have been young couples who became disillusioned with their former careers. The Hendricksons' ability to relate to young people is nowhere more apparent than in their own home. "Humor and understanding bounce between the parents and their five children like tennis balls," wrote one associate, "reminding onlookers that both Hendricksons began careers in education."

The family-oriented life-style of John and Pat is evident in their home, a place of warm decor, which is always filled with what they describe as their "favorite hobby" — people. Among those frequently present are, of course, those very active distributors who are also members of their own family.

"HUMOR AND UNDERSTANDING": OPPOSITE, *Crown Ambassador Direct Distributors John and Pat Hendrickson.* TOP LEFT, *the Hendricksons featured on the cover of the January 1981* Amagram. TOP RIGHT AND CENTER, *the spotlight's on, as the Hendrickson family is interviewed for an Amway video.* BOTTOM LEFT, *showing off a special bedspread.* BOTTOM RIGHT, *John and Pat with son David and daughters Jill, JoAnn, Mary, and Susan.*

Howard and Faye Vaughan, Crown Direct Distributors from California, also fall into the "family heritage" category. Their son, Stephen, is an Amway distributor; one daughter, Debbie, is a full-time secretary for the Vaughans' office; and another daughter, Melinda, is married to Thadius Morton, an Amway distributor. Their two youngest daughters, Joanna and Martha, started helping with the family Amway business when they were in their teens.

Other distributors who have passed along the Amway torch to the second generation include Dan and Bunny Williams of California; Vince and Alice Gaffey of Illinois; Bernice Hansen of Michigan; and Sterling and Evangeline Krause of Minnesota. Yet they are only a few of those who symbolize the uniqueness of the Amway opportunity as a truly family-oriented business.

PASSING THE TORCH: RIGHT, Crown Direct Distributors Howard and Faye Vaughan. BELOW, the Vaughans in Ada on their Double Diamond Day.

THE GOAL OF PERSONAL INDEPENDENCE

The *Washington Post* once editorialized, "Amway merchandises free enterprise as aggressively as it sells soap."

The comment was half correct. Few would deny that the company resolutely defends the cause of free enterprise. Yet no one in Amway's management would agree with the implication that "selling soap" is the company's prime function. Although soap products do indeed figure prominently in the marketing programs, along with other lines, they are not as vital as the intangible commodity that distributors seek: *opportunity*.

Opportunity has been referred to in one book about Amway as "The Possible Dream." The dream becomes reality through the Sales and Marketing Plan, not simply a formula for selling products, but a blueprint for owning and operating an independent business. The essentials include financial independence, the chance to be your own boss, freedom from punching a time clock, and very often a second income.

Jim and Margaret Floor, Diamond Direct Distributors from California, are good examples of the independence and success that can come from Amway. After 16 years as an executive with a major corporation, Jim resigned to spend full time as an Amway distributor. The reason: He had already seen, after four years as a part-time distributor, that he could get away from a nine-to-five workday and improve his income as well.

"Instead of the negative, dog-eat-dog attitude of a loner and a fighter climbing the corporate ladder," explains Jim, "I found that success in Amway is based on helping other people achieve success. My attitude changed from one of jealous competition to helping and cheering others on to their own goals and successes."

"CHEERING OTHERS ON": TOP, the September 1979 Amagram *featured Crown Ambassador Direct Distributors Dan and Bunny Williams.* CENTER, *Crown Direct Distributor Bernice Hansen.* BOTTOM, *Jim and Margaret Floor, Diamond Direct Distributors.*

Amway has sometimes been criticized for the emphasis it places, in sales literature and at rallies, on some of the material rewards of success. Mention is made, for example, of being able to live in better communities, afford a more comfortable home, trade in the old car for a new model, travel more often, or win valuable prizes for achieving sales goals. Acknowledging that these improvements in life-style are possible for people who join Amway, DeVos points out that rewards should hardly be cause for guilt.

"Success is not sinful," he asserts, emphasizing that Amway distributors, both as individuals and as a group, demonstrate great responsibility as private citizens. They support their churches, their communities, and those charitable organizations they feel are particularly deserving. They are active as civic volunteers, participating in charity fund-raising dinners, hospital benefits, youth programs, and other local activities. They serve on educational boards, hold nonpaying positions in town government, help train Scouts, and otherwise devote their time and talents to the good of their neighbors.

"I know a lot of very giving Amway distributors who are involved in all sorts of charitable activities," says Ruby Direct Distributor Mary Jo Chojnowski, "but most of them don't broadcast it." As an example, she points to the 1984 Easter Seals Telethon. Amway distributors, many of whom volunteered to staff the phones and record pledges, helped to raise more than one million dollars — the single largest contribution ever received by the Easter Seals Foundation from a first-time organizational sponsor.

Significantly, the check was presented by Executive Diamond Direct Distributors John and Jennie Belle Crowe to Easter Seals host Pat Boone, himself an Amway distributor. One of the reasons distributors have been so successful in raising money for charitable purposes is that they know how to communicate such needs to their fellow citizens. In Pennsylvania, for example, Diamond Direct Distributors Scott and Lynne Shaw and Dan and Mary Bell, along with their group, organized a gigantic "Bowl-A-Thon" for Easter Seals and received pledges totaling more than $40,000.

One Diamond Direct Distributor who has helped thousands of needy people around the globe in a completely different way is Doug Wead of Missouri. With his wife, Gloria, he helped to organize the Washington Charity Dinner, now an annual event, to honor individuals for their charity work. The event began as an effort in 1979 to provide relief to Cambodian refugees. At that time, the Weads met with distributors Pat and Shirley Boone in the home of Nancy and Ronald Reagan to determine how to organize a lifesaving program in Cambodia. Since then the Charity Dinner has raised more than half a million dollars for Cambodian relief, $100,000 for drug rehabilitation, and more than a million dollars for food for starving refugees in Central America.

In 1984, the City of Hope National Medical Center and Research Institute bestowed its "Spirit of Life" award to Dan and Bunny Williams, Crown Ambassador Direct Distributors. This award, which recognizes outstanding humanitarianism, was presented to the Williamses during a testimonial dinner in Los Angeles. Over 600 people attended the gala and Rich DeVos was among the featured speakers. Proceeds from the dinner established the Dan and Bunny Williams Research Fellowship in the City of Hope, a hospital in Duarte, California, which treats catastrophic diseases free of charge.

HELPING HANDS: OPPOSITE, TOP, Ruby Direct Distributor Mary Jo Chojnowski and husband Larry. OPPOSITE, CENTER, Amway President Rich DeVos with actor Richard Thomas at the 1984 Easter Seals Telethon. OPPOSITE, BOTTOM, Pat Boone chats with Direct Distributors Ed and Barb Morton, Pearl Direct Distributors Ken and Shirley Goss, and Rich DeVos. ABOVE, Diamond Direct Distributors Doug and Gloria Wead, organizers of the annual Washington Charity Dinner. TOP RIGHT, Dan and Bunny Williams, Crown Ambassador Direct Distributors, are honored with the 1984 "Spirit of Life" Award by the City of Hope National Medical Center and Research Institute in California. BOTTOM RIGHT, (left to right) Diamond Direct Distributors Scott and Lynne Shaw and Mary and Dan Bell with Rich DeVos and host Pat Boone at the 1985 Easter Seals Telethon.

SANTA'S ELVES: Each year Diamond Directs Elmer and Jamie Gibson, with their distributors' help, host a daylong Christmas party for orphans from local youth shelters in their hometown of Henderson, Kentucky.

Other examples of this brand of good citizenship among Amway distributors are Elmer and Jamie Gibson, Diamond Directs from Henderson, Kentucky, who invited their distributors to help them host a daylong Christmas party for 100 orphans from local youth shelters; Max and Lorraine Butterfield, who contribute their time to establishing soup kitchens in Maryland that feed about 800 needy people each month; and Edna Dougherty who, with her husband, Jack, devoted so much time over the years to the March of Dimes and the American Cancer Society that the mayor of her home town of Austin, Texas, proclaimed Edna Dougherty Day in her honor and presented her with an award for "Service to Mankind."

INCENTIVES: THE FUEL OF SUCCESS

While pointing to the public service records of typical distributors, Jay Van Andel and Rich DeVos make it clear that they are in no way apologizing for Amway's policies of motivating people with the promise of rewards that they consider worth striving for. "Material rewards are the incentives that fuel the free enterprise society," emphasizes DeVos.

Company literature itself reflects this viewpoint: "Amway distributors are volunteers. They cannot be motivated by force. They can be motivated only by rewards of achievement, money, status, recognition, and the realization of goals. But this type of motivation is the best there is; in all of human history it has always brought about the highest achievement."

The automobile awards program is a case in point, using the slogan "You have the drive — Amway has the car." Those who strive to win this reward are unanimous in their praise for this type of incentive, and yet they are the kinds of family-oriented, community-loving couples who appreciate the intangible and spiritual values of life as well as the material ones.

"Earning the car was a turning point," say Justin and Beverly Baker, Ruby Direct Distributors from Iowa. "Amway's been good to us and it has helped us to be able to raise our children happily. It takes a great group to succeed, with someone out front leading the way."

"The car program was a definite goal we could see in front of us and work toward," say Michigan's Wally and Norma Buttrick. "It probably was the one single thing that made our business grow. We believe it's one of the best promotions Amway has ever had."

In person, on tapes, and in his writings, DeVos radiates optimism as he advocates the philosophy summed up in his two favorite words, "*I can!*" As he has often said, "We have been given the power to change our condition. Set a goal, decide to pursue it, and know it will require hard work. Believe in yourself and aim high. Almost anyone can do whatever he really believes he can."

Although the founders and others who have been with Amway for many years respect their business heritage, "yesterday" has far less impact in the scheme of things than "today" and "tomorrow." Amway, explains retired executive vice president Orville Hoxie, "is not satisfied with yesterday's accomplishments. We're interested in what we can do today and tomorrow. It is not enough to stand on your achievements — you must look forward and move on." That spirit, Hoxie adds, "has animated the business and is at the core of its success."

Another hallmark of the Amway philosophy is its commitment to human dignity and individual worth. DeVos himself has emphasized this viewpoint as a recurring theme in his speeches and writings. "It's great to be a salesperson," he has often assured his audiences and readers. "Sales generate all the income there is. To call yourself 'just a salesperson' is to deny your own worth. The most important commodity in the world is respect for the individual, and the persons who do their jobs with pride and competence strengthen the backbone of this country. They are the ones who get the job done, the unsung heroes of our society."

Clearly illustrating this point are Simon and Elaine Blouin, distributors from Quebec. "We were financially strong before we joined Amway, so money and security didn't inspire us," explains Simon, who for five consecutive years had earned coveted membership in the Million Dollar Club of the Bank of Montreal.

Why, then, did he abandon an eminent position as a banker to go into sales?

The answer is that he and his wife both yearned for something that had been lacking: personal recognition. Simon recalled their first attendance at a rally, where they were caught up in the excitement of recognition. "The speaker was treated like a star, and that's what I wanted."

KEEPING THE FAITH: OPPOSITE, Helen DeVos, honorary chairperson of Grand Rapids' Toys for Tots campaign, with local TV personality Dick Richards (left), and local businessman Bernie Morey. ABOVE, Simon and Elaine Blouin, Diamond Direct Distributors from Quebec. TOP RIGHT, Chairman Van Andel addresses a 1986 meeting of the Diamond Club. BOTTOM RIGHT, Betty Van Andel and shipyard owner John Van Lent at the christening of Enterprise IV in the Netherlands.

Needless to say, as Diamond Direct Distributors, the Blouins have received accolades that are all but unknown to people in other types of careers. The recognition even began rubbing off on their young son, François. "He can see we are successful by the letters and phone calls we get and by seeing us recognized in rallies, which was not true in the banking business .... Now François wants recognition, too. He is the goalie on his hockey team and he plays to win. He hasn't lost a game yet!"

That is the kind of spirit that passes down from distributor to distributor, and even from one generation to the next. Its concept is zealously protected in all corporate decisions relating to the

people in the field. Company policy has always been shaped to assure favorable development of the distributor. As Orville Hoxie notes, "The corporation does not make decisions that improve the internal side of operations at the distributors' expense."

Retired Executive Vice President Gordon Teska recalls what he thought was a creative suggestion: A substantial sum could be saved by the marketing administrative office if a business form were revised. The proposal was turned down flat: It would have meant additional paperwork for distributors.

Building faith between the company and its distributors and maintaining internal faith with its people is a concept that management bears constantly in mind. DeVos recalls his own father's counsel after the new company had been in operation for several years. "He said that the foundation of the company had been honesty and fairness in our dealings, that people had come to count on Amway and what it stood for, and that I should not let them down. I have never forgotten that wisdom."

Communication is the key to fair, open dealings between individuals and groups at corporate headquarters. Van Andel and DeVos, very much in evidence and well-regarded, constantly return the affection and respect of their employees. Monthly "Speak-Up" sessions, during which employees meet with DeVos and other executives, keep the dialogue flowing in both directions. Initiated by the president and chairman in the 1960s to make sure that everyone had a chance to be heard, the early sessions were attended by groups of employees that were rotated so that over a period of time "all employees would have a chance to listen to me and me to them," says DeVos.

The size of the corporation and the everyday commitments of management in other locations have changed the complexion of these once more-personal sessions. Yet "Speak-Up" meetings continue, with representative selections of employees from the various departments voicing their concerns and presenting improvement suggestions. "These meetings let people know they are being heard," explains DeVos, "and that each person is judged important."

Further evidence of the company's policies regarding employees can be seen in its pension and profit-sharing plans and other benefit programs, recreational facilities, and various additional "perks," the perquisites that label Amway as having a favorable career environment. A workplace without a union, Amway has been the site of a few attempts to organize — efforts that have always fizzled. On one occasion when several truck drivers attempted to create some interest in a union, they typically failed to collect enough signatures to hold an election.

"We are outspoken on the rights of any employees to do whatever they have in mind," emphasizes DeVos, "including membership in a union. But we are equally outspoken in voicing the opinion that no one should be required to pay someone else for the privilege of working. That's a distinct loss of freedom. We believe that this country supports the right of each person to join or not to join, to belong or not to belong."

SUPPORTING: MORE THAN GOOD BUSINESS

Recognizing the value of America's heritage and the necessity to preserve her culture, Amway has long supported the arts as a corporate responsibility. In tribute to the nation's "unsung heroes," the company in 1984 commissioned a series of 25 paintings by Michigan artist Paul Collins. Collectively entitled "America at Work," the canvases portray a representative selection of workers, from actor to astronaut, newspaper deliverer to neurosurgeon. First exhibited at the United States Department of Labor in Washington and now on permanent display at the Amway Grand Plaza Hotel in Grand Rapids, the exhibition commemorates freedom, equal opportunity, and respect for achievement.

One part of the company's patronage of the arts has been the sponsorship and commissioning of artists on works in progress. Michigan artist Armand Merizon was commissioned for two years by the company to paint a variety of pictures showcasing his broad talents. The collection was then displayed in various cities, adding to the artist's national renown. Another series, rendered by nationally famous etcher Reynold Weidenaar, consists of sketches in the headquarters collection that depict Amway manufacturing processes, as well as a collection in the Amway Grand Plaza Hotel showing its construction.

In 1982, in honor of the Netherlands-American Bicentennial Celebration, chaired by Jay Van Andel, Amway sponsored a yearlong exhibit at Amsterdam's Stedelijk Museum, one of Europe's leading centers of modern art. The exhibit, using the theme "Young American Artists," featured works by four of America's most promising contemporary painters: Neil Jenney, Julian Schnabel, Susan Rothenberg, and Robert Mangold. Displaying a completely different kind of creativity, Amway sponsored a float on behalf of the Netherlands-American Bicentennial Commission as an entry in the 1982 Tournament of Roses parade. Entitled "Hands Across the Sea," it was awarded the International Trophy for the event.

PATRONS OF THE ARTS: *ABOVE, artist Paul Collins with Amway's owners at the opening of his "America at Work" collection in the Amway Grand Plaza Hotel.* TOP RIGHT, *the DeVos family welcomes Queen Beatrix and Prince Claus of the Netherlands to Grand Rapids.* CENTER, *Jay and Betty Van Andel with Queen Beatrix and Prince Claus at the Celebration of Praise and Thanksgiving, during the 1982 royal visit to western Michigan as part of the Netherlands-American Bicentennial Celebration.* BOTTOM LEFT, *the award-winning Amway-sponsored "Hands Across the Sea" float, entered in the 1982 Tournament of Roses parade by the Netherlands-American Bicentennial Commission.* BOTTOM RIGHT, *Jay Van Andel, chairman of the 1982 Netherlands-American Bicentennial Commission, and wife Betty are greeted by President Ronald Reagan at the White House reception for Queen Beatrix of the Netherlands.*

On a broader scale, Van Andel and DeVos have contributed generously to a wide range of local cultural projects and institutions, personally as well as through the company. Beneficiaries have included the Grand Rapids Art Museum, the Arts Council of Greater Grand Rapids, and the Gerald R. Ford Presidential Museum. The city's DeVos Hall for the Performing Arts, dedicated in 1980, was named for Richard and Helen DeVos, its principal benefactors. A personal love of music led the DeVoses, through the Richard and Helen DeVos Foundation, to sponsor the DeVos Quartet, first-chair string section of the Grand Rapids Symphony Orchestra. Amway, too, has contributed substantially to the Symphony, as well as to other local musical events and fund-raising appeals. The Van Andels are substantial supporters of the Grand Rapids Opera and Betty Van Andel is a member of that board.

Corporate sponsorship of the arts, however, is by no means limited to local institutions and talents. In 1983, Amway funded an American tour of the Hong Kong Children's Choir. It financed that year's debut and the continuing operation of the Malaysian Youth Symphony Orchestra. One year earlier, it had sponsored the European tour of the National Symphony Orchestra under the baton of the renowned Mstislav Rostropovich. For its support of the NSO tour and the Stedelijk Museum exhibit, the Amway Corporation was honored with the prestigious 1983 "Business in the Arts Award."

While support for the arts stems from the inherent cultural interests of the founders of the company, it is also a sound business investment. The Netherlands, Malaysia, Hong Kong, Canada, and the nations selected for the National Symphony Orchestra tours all contain Amway affiliates. As a result, patronage in these countries has positioned the company as a concerned corporate citizen and stimulated justifiable pride among distributors within their borders.

These many outside contributions by Amway to charitable organizations, to civic and community programs, to the arts, and to the betterment of the environments in which it operates have earned the company a name and stature second to none in the corporate business world.

A JOYFUL NOISE: OPPOSITE, TOP, *Amway's co-founders in conversation with renowned cellist and conductor of the National Symphony Orchestra Mstislav Rostropovich.* OPPOSITE, CENTER, *Rostropovich joins the DeVoses in the Amway Board Room; (left to right) Doug, Dan, Rich, and Helen DeVos, Rostropovich, Betsy and Dick DeVos.* OPPOSITE, BOTTOM, *Jay Van Andel, chairman of the U.S. Chamber of Commerce from 1979-80, addressing a Chamber of Commerce meeting.* TOP LEFT, *Mstislav Rostropovich performing at an Amway employee concert in the Center of Free Enterprise Auditorium.* TOP RIGHT, *the Hong Kong Children's Choir on their 1983 Amway-sponsored American tour.* CENTER RIGHT, *Hong Kong Children's Choir member Wong Sun Tat demonstrates the ancient erhu for Scott and Jeff, sons of choir hosts Burl and Joan Simmons.* BOTTOM LEFT, *Amway treats the young choir members to a picnic in a Los Angeles park.* BOTTOM RIGHT, *choir members pose with a new friend at Disneyland.*

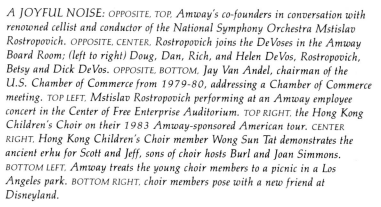

Amway's President Rich DeVos and Chairman Jay Van Andel in 1986.

Conclusion

VISION FOR TOMORROW

*"We dare not just look back to
great yesterdays. We must
look forward to great
tomorrows."*
— *Adlai E. Stevenson*

Nearly a century ago, British historian Lord Bryce startled some of his readers by asserting that on the other side of the Atlantic the most creative citizens were not America's artists but her businessmen.

Many years later, popular opinion in the United States began to echo this opinion as creativity was discovered to be one of the driving forces behind such noted entrepreneurs as John D. Rockefeller, Andrew Carnegie, and Henry Ford. Turning opportunity into achievement was proven to be more dependent upon imagination and innovation than upon management formulas and financial statistics.

Jay Van Andel and Rich DeVos may not immediately have recognized the truth of this somewhat unconventional concept when they started to develop Amway, but they soon learned that they were doing something right as they watched their efforts take root. What they were doing from the very start was creatively developing a concept of selling that, while not new in the historical sense, was gloriously alive and innovative.

Van Andel once spoke of the "watersheds" that occur in the life of every business, beginning with the initial entrepreneurial period when the founders ran a "hands-on shop, doing a lot of everything." The course of many young companies never flows beyond this initial watershed because the next level requires the imagination to transfer certain decision-making capabilities to other people.

DeVos parallels this figure of speech by defining four such watersheds in the company's growth. The first covered a "scrambling period," characterized by "the bringing together of people with an idea and the testing of it to see if it will fly." For Amway, this period lasted for two or three years into the 1960s. The second watershed was broader, a period of "building the corporate structure" that spanned ten or twelve years, lasting into the late 1970s. The third level was represented by the early 1980s and the challenges of "a maturing organization, very much like the period that parents go through when their teenagers pull away from them." He points out that this was a risky period because there was a tendency for people to pull in several directions to develop their own interests or, worse yet, to become complacent. Needed to offset such negative trends were creative ideas, innovation, and watchful planning.

The fourth "watershed" is, of course, the present and future when Amway will achieve "a new wave of excitement and growth as new people all over the world discover and rediscover the Amway opportunity."

THE GIFT OF CREATIVITY

Inherent in the Amway concept is the kind of individual creativity that makes it possible for distributors to stimulate and motivate others in a manner that cannot be achieved through routine contacting and selling. Consider, for example, the brief item contributed by one distributor and printed in an early issue of *Amagram* magazine, displaying a highly imaginative and certainly creative approach to selling.

HOORAY ! IT'S SNOWING (OR POURING) !!

What a wonderful day for Amway selling. Nearly everybody will be at home, planning to stay at home, catching up on extra cleaning jobs. I'll have a chance to talk to some prospects I haven't been able to tie down before.

And I have some wonderful bad-weather products to sell: Amway dri-fab, Shoe Glo, Chrome and Glass Cleaner.... It's a wonderful day for cleaning the oven, polishing the silver, shampooing the rugs. And I've got what those jobs take.

This ought to be a day with that extra time in it for a promising pitch on Queen Cookware. Bad-weather days are good selling days for Amway and me.

PORTRAIT OF PROGRESS: 25th Anniversary Mural by Paul Collins, presented as a gift to Jay Van Andel and Rich DeVos by the U.S. and Canadian Amway Distributors Associations. Dedicated at Amway's 1985 Annual Convention, the mural is now on permanent display in the Center of Free Enterprise.

A whimsical example of creativity was a bit of verse penned by the late Bunny Marks. Bunny and her husband, Dick, were Amway's first Crown Ambassadors.

Get up in the morning and clap your hands,
Don't say you can't when you know you can.
Turn on the shower and let it run,
This is your day for work and fun!
Before breakfast, kiss your honey,
Your attitude can make you money.
When a go-light you see,
Say that goal is for me!
The ones you sponsor won't be few
Because you offer life anew.
Whatever your dreams, they can come true,
It depends on one person ... that person is YOU!

In Amway, you don't have to be a Shakespeare or Michelangelo or Beethoven to put imagination and creativity to productive use. The ingenious little touches and the innovative ways of going about what might otherwise be a routine task make all the difference. Sometimes sales creativity is as simple as the strategy used by Mike and Judy Pittman of Alabama.

"We offer a gift-shopping service that has been our most successful program," said Judy. "We make up a list of people, like aunts, uncles, teachers, just to jog our memories. Then we remind customers well before Christmas and other important holidays and anniversaries, providing gift suggestions as well.

"We ask them to check off the people they want to buy gifts for and how much they want to spend. Then we make three or four gift suggestions from our regular line or from the Personal Shoppers Catalog. We emphasize that they can do their shopping without ever walking out the door!"

Few people in Amway, or any other business, have shown more creativity and ingenuity than Paul and Linda Blicharz, of Maryland. As Amway's first deaf Direct Distributors, they are pioneers in opening up immense new opportunities for the deaf.

"This is the only business in the world that gives deaf people an opportunity to develop an income equal to, or better than, that of people who can hear," said Paul. "Deaf people have been told for so long that they can't do this or that. They've been overprotected and in some cases have been regarded as mentally retarded. They've grown up that way and now they have to work on that negative self-image. We're trying to change their thinking from 'I can't' to 'I can.'"

His concept that deaf people can succeed in a business like Amway's has been well-supported by the results. The Blicharzes' own group in Maryland includes more than 200 deaf distributors, as well as people who can hear.

"One thing about a Blicharz meeting," observed a journalist who covered the proceedings and watched the "finger chatter" of the deaf members, "is that the neighbors can never complain about any noise!"

No matter how you look at it, creativity is a driving force that keeps the Amway tradition vigorous and healthy from one generation to the next. But how can you depict such nebulous concepts as guidelines for the future when "creativity" and "vision" can mean so many different things to different people?

One story that has numerous versions, though all with the same conclusion, tells about the little boy in the fourth grade who seemed to be having trouble relating to his classmates. Whenever he was belittled because of his shabby clothing or rustic idiom, he would sooner or later start talking about his home. It had, he insisted, a backyard that was endless, "longer than any of you could really dream of." His classmates simply snickered, for one look at the boy showed that he came from a poor home that could not have much to offer, let alone expansive acreage.

One day, the teacher had occasion to visit the home to confer with the mother and father. Afterwards, she asked her pupil if he would show her the wondrous backyard he had so often talked about. He eagerly led her out the kitchen door — to a tiny cubicle of seared grass and scraggly flowers, hemmed in by other buildings.

"But I thought you said it was endless!" she stammered, momentarily chagrined that the poor little boy had been telling a fib all this time.

"Oh it *is* !" he exclaimed, pointing eagerly to the sky. "It stretches all the way up to the stars, and sometimes even to the moon!"

That little boy had vision, as well as a concept of the future. He was not about to let cramped quarters and confining walls restrict his outlook on life. It was an equal degree of farsightedness that enhanced the outlook of Jay Van Andel and Rich DeVos during that first year of Amway when the company was literally encased within the confines of two cluttered

basements. And it is this same kind of vision that has made it possible for hundreds of thousands of Amway distributors to look beyond the normal confines of life and find boundless freedom. It has made it possible for their children — and now even some of their grandchildren — to benefit from foresight rather than having to be regretful over hindsight.

THE NEXT GENERATION

Applying their own creative and visionary capacities to the work of their fathers and mothers, the next generation of Van Andels and DeVoses shares the excitement and growth of the Amway opportunity. "One of the greatest challenges facing a private, family-owned business," acknowledges Jay Van Andel, "is how it integrates the next generation."

In 1977, recognizing that the eldest children, Dick DeVos and Nan Van Andel, had reached their early twenties and were ready to assume a substantial role in the company's future, Amway's owners called in their longtime consultant, Clair Knox, to plan a management training program. The objective: "To have the second generation qualified to carry on the well-established philosophy so carefully emphasized and practiced by the founders."

The result was a unique, effective plan that utilized the company's own precept that *the best teacher is experience*. The five-year training period was designed to expose the upcoming generation to all aspects of the corporation and at the same time provide opportunities to focus on areas of special interest. Nan and Dick were the first to complete the program, leaving the way open for their brothers and sisters: Dan, Cheri, and Doug DeVos, and Steve, Dave, and Barbara Van Andel.

Dick and Nan especially grew up with Amway. They clearly remember the people who came to work in the family basements, including Kay Evans who served as secretary, but was skilled at making "the best paper airplanes." Both spent time during high school and college vacations working in the plant and other locations, including stints at Mutual Broadcasting, Nutrilite, and distribution centers. When they entered the formal training program, they studied each function in much greater detail, as "hands-on people," rather than observers. Wherever possible, concentration was on the planning and administrative aspects of the operations.

More vital than acquiring data about such details as manufacturing processes, reports Dick, was getting to understand employees — their motivations, challenges, problems, and roles in the company — "valuable knowledge in years to come."

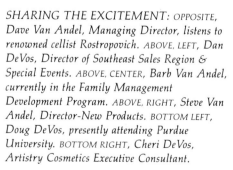

SHARING THE EXCITEMENT: OPPOSITE, Dave Van Andel, Managing Director, listens to renowned cellist Rostropovich. ABOVE, LEFT, Dan DeVos, Director of Southeast Sales Region & Special Events. ABOVE, CENTER, Barb Van Andel, currently in the Family Management Development Program. ABOVE, RIGHT, Steve Van Andel, Director-New Products. BOTTOM LEFT, Doug DeVos, presently attending Purdue University. BOTTOM RIGHT, Cheri DeVos, Artistry Cosmetics Executive Consultant.

From the time Nan worked as a child assembling Nutrilite sample kits, she knew that one day she would join the company. Shortly after college, she began her training, working on assignments that ranged from loading trucks to organizing personnel records, to composing press releases. "The experience was fun," she notes, "but they didn't spare us any pain. We had to do pretty much of everything."

Nan and Dick also spent time as actual Amway distributors, doing what every distributor does: selling products, sponsoring distributors, building a business. Though they had grown up with Amway, to run their own distributorships provided Dick and Nan with invaluable experience and a broadened perspective.

At the corporation, the training program not only served its basic educational purpose but has proved to be an objective for the younger Van Andels and DeVoses as they follow the same footsteps. Upon completion of their training, Nan and Dick moved into key positions in communications, the former as editor of *Amagram* magazine and *Newsgram*, and the latter assuming responsibility for corporate meetings. Both have been appointed vice presidents, DeVos for Amway International and Van Andel for Communications, and are serving on the Policy Committee as well.

"HANDS-ON PEOPLE": ABOVE, Nan Van Andel and Pat Boone at the 1985 Annual Convention in Grand Rapids. TOP RIGHT, Nan Van Andel. BOTTOM RIGHT, Dick DeVos.

CHANGE AND DEVELOPMENT

The company administered by this next generation will see many changes in the Amway of the future. Consistent with their philosophy that a well-run business must continually evolve, Jay Van Andel and Rich DeVos have regularly consolidated and increased the efficiency of all corporate operations. One key to this constant revitalizing process is the position of coordinator of planning and policy, currently held by William Nicholson. DeVos and Van Andel had first met Nicholson when he was appointments secretary for President Gerald Ford, himself a longtime friend of Amway.

Discovering a shared enthusiasm for business, they asked Nicholson to open and administer a Government Affairs Office for the company in Washington, after President Ford had left the White House. In 1984, Nicholson, who had also assisted in the acquisition of Mutual Broadcasting in 1977, was asked to rejoin Amway as coordinator. Specifically, he was charged with the responsibility of reviewing all phases of company operations and recommending procedures to assure clearer lines of accountability.

TODAY'S AMWAY: *ABOVE, Dick DeVos discusses international marketing strategy with Amway consultant General Alexander Haig. BELOW, LEFT, Otto Stolz, Executive Vice President of Amway Corporation. BELOW, RIGHT, Bill Nicholson, Amway's Chief Operating Officer.*

As always, in the process of strengthening the company, Jay Van Andel and Rich DeVos continue to set the tone. Both foresee an exciting future as Amway faces interesting new challenges and becomes increasingly significant on both the domestic and international scene. "I would like to see a company spread over the world," asserts DeVos, "spreading our heritage as our children take new and leading roles in carrying on what we have begun."

The members of the new generation, sharing the vision and creativity of their elders, accept this role with pride and determination. Speaking for her peers, Nan Van Andel has likened Amway to a social phenomenon. "You have to want Amway to go on," she observes, "not for your own self-interest, but because Amway helps people to help themselves. The Amway opportunity has been a godsend for the millions of people whose lives have been touched by this business, and who have discovered something of value that they could never have found anywhere else."

ON STAGE: *The second generation of Van Andels and DeVoses gather on stage at the 1985 Annual Convention.*

GALLERY OF ACHIEVEMENT

CROWN AMBASSADOR DIRECT DISTRIBUTORS

Crown Ambassador Direct Distributors have achieved the highest business level in the World of Amway. To qualify, a distributor must personally sponsor twenty (or more) 25% groups, each of which was at the 25% Performance Bonus level at least six months of the fiscal year.

DALLAS & BETTY BEAIRD
California
Amway distributors since 1965
Achieved Crown Ambassador Direct Dist. in 1980

FRANK & RITA DELISLE
California
Amway distributors since 1962
Achieved Crown Ambassador Direct Dist. in 1980

JOHN & PAT HENDRICKSON
California
Amway distributors since 1965
Achieved Crown Ambassador Direct Dist. in 1980

JIM & SHARON JANZ
British Columbia
Amway distributors since 1964
Achieved Crown Ambassador Direct Dist. in 1978

DICK & SANDEE MARKS
Minnesota
Amway distributors since 1965
Achieved Crown Ambassador Direct Dist. in 1977

CHARLIE & ELSIE MARSH
Florida
Amway distributors since 1964
Achieved Crown Ambassador Direct Dist. in 1979

BOB & JOYCE SCHMIDT
British Columbia
Amway distributors since 1974
Achieved Crown Ambassador Direct Dist. in 1981

CHUCK & JEAN STREHLI
Texas
Amway distributors since 1965
Achieved Crown Ambassador Direct Dist. in 1979

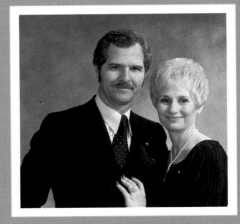

JERRY & SHARYN WEBB
Texas
Amway distributors since 1969
Achieved Crown Ambassador Direct Dist. in 1979

DAN & BUNNY WILLIAMS
California
Amway distributors since 1966
Achieved Crown Ambassador Direct Dist. in 1979

ROBERT & NICOLE BELLI
France
Amway distributors since 1978
Achieved Crown Ambassador Direct Dist. in 1985

JOE & FRANCE MAS
France
Amway distributors since 1977
Achieved Crown Ambassador Direct Dist. in 1982

**DR. PETER & EVA
MUELLER-MEERKATZ**
West Germany
Amway distributors since 1976
Achieved Crown Ambassador Direct Dist. in 1979

MAX & MARIANNE SCHWARZ
West Germany
Amway distributors since 1977
Achieved Crown Ambassador Direct Dist. in 1982

MICHAEL & GABY STRACHOWITZ
West Germany
Amway distributors since 1977
Achieved Crown Ambassador Direct Dist. in 1982

CROWN DIRECT DISTRIBUTORS

Crown Direct Distributors have established themselves as top achievers in the World of Amway. To qualify, a distributor must sponsor at least eighteen 25% groups, each of which was at the 25% Performance Bonus level at least six months of the fiscal year.

BOB & TERRY ANDREWS
Florida
Amway distributors since 1972
Achieved Crown Direct Dist. in 1980

WAYNE & KAY BEAIRD
California
Amway distributors since 1965
Achieved Crown Direct Dist. in 1978

DENNIS & KAY BEECHER
California
Amway distributors since 1970
Achieved Crown Direct Dist. in 1978

ANDRE & FRANCOISE BLANCHARD
Quebec
Amway distributors since 1967
Achieved Crown Direct Dist. in 1980

CECILE CHAPDELAINE
Quebec
Amway distributor since 1973
Achieved Crown Direct Dist. in 1977

ART & OLLIE CHARLTON
Florida
Amway distributors since 1965
Achieved Crown Direct Dist. in 1970

DAVID & NADIA COMYNS
Australia
Amway distributors since 1971
Achieved Crown Direct Dist. in 1979

JIM & NANCY DORNAN
California
Amway distributors since 1970
Achieved Crown Direct Dist. in 1979

JERE & EILEEN DUTT
JODY & GINA DUTT
Ohio
Amway distributors since 1959
Achieved Crown Direct Dist. in 1979

STAN & RUTH EVANS
Colorado
Amway distributors since 1965
Achieved Crown Direct Dist. in 1978

BERNICE HANSEN
SKIP & SUE ROSS
Michigan
Amway distributors since 1959
Achieved Crown Direct Dist. in 1975

GRANT & MARCELLA HEDGPETH
California
Amway distributors since 1968
Achieved Crown Direct Dist. in 1979

JERRY & ESTHER HICKS
Arizona
Amway distributors since 1969
Achieved Crown Direct Dist. in 1979

TRISH HICKS
Tennessee
Amway distributor since 1969
Achieved Crown Direct Dist. in 1979

DAVE & CAROL KENDALL
California
Amway distributors since 1970
Achieved Crown Direct Dist. in 1979

STERLING & VAN KRAUSE
ROGER & RUTH KRAUSE
Minnesota
Amway distributors since 1959
Achieved Crown Direct Dist. in 1971

VERN & JUDY MORSE
Michigan
Amway distributors since 1969
Achieved Crown Direct Dist. in 1980

DICK & DEE OSSINGER
Washington
Amway distributors since 1965
Achieved Crown Direct Dist. in 1979

GORDON & EDIE ROSS
British Columbia
Amway distributors since 1964
Achieved Crown Direct Dist. in 1973

WALLY & JOANNE SOUSA
Oregon
Amway distributors since 1970
Achieved Crown Direct Dist. in 1980

V. HOWARD & FAYE VAUGHAN
California
Amway distributors since 1965
Achieved Crown Direct Dist. in 1979

RON, HELYNE & JOE VICTOR
Ohio
Amway distributors since 1959
Achieved Crown Direct Dist. in 1979

JODY & KATHY VICTOR
Ohio
Amway distributors since 1968
Achieved Crown Direct Dist. in 1981

DEXTER & BIRDIE YAGER
North Carolina
Amway distributors since 1964
Achieved Crown Direct Dist. in 1981

172

INDEX